From Acorns

How to build a brilliant business

Caspian Woods

Second edition

PEARSON
Prentice Hall
BUSINESS

an imprint of Pearson Education
Harlow, England • London • New York • Toronto • Sydney •
Tokyo • Singapore • Hong Kong • Cape Town • New Delhi •
Madrid • Paris • Amsterdam • Munich • Milan

PEARSON EDUCATION LIMITED

Edinburgh Gate
Harlow CM20 2JE
Tel: +44 (0)1279 623623
Fax: +44 (0)1279 431059
www.pearsoned.co.uk

First published in Great Britain in 2004
Second edition published 2007

© Caspian Woods 2004, 2007

The right of Caspian Woods to be identified as author of this work has been
asserted by him in accordance with the Copyright, Designs and Patents Act 1988.

ISBN: 978-0-273-71252-7

British Library Cataloguing-in-Publication Data
A catalogue record for this book is available from the British Library

All rights reserved. No part of this publication may be reproduced, stored in a
retrieval system, or transmitted in any form or by any means, electronic, mechan-
ical, photocopying, recording or otherwise, without either the prior written
permission of the Publisher or a licence permitting restricted copying in the
United Kingdom issued by the Copyright Licensing Agency Ltd, Saffron House,
6–10 Kirby Street, London EC1N 8TS. This book may not be lent, resold, hired
out or otherwise disposed of by way of trade in any form of binding or cover other
than that in which it is published, without the prior consent of the Publishers.

10 9 8 7 6 5 4 3 2 1
11 10 09 08 07

Typeset in 9.5pt Melior by 3
Printed and bound in Great Britain by Ashford Colour Press, Gosport

The publisher's policy is to use paper manufactured from sustainable forests.

BELFAST EDUCATION AND LIBRARY BOARD	
C111086309	
Bertrams	25.02.08
658.11WOO	£9.99
	G070132

Dedicated to Christopher Woods

Contents

The entrepreneur's ten commandments

1. Get selling

Business is not rocket science. If you've got plenty of people buying things from you for more than they cost you, you are most of the way there. There are many distractions along the way, but you should always be spending *at least* 50 per cent of your time selling.

2. Strive to be different

There is a lot of noise out there, and a lot of big boring companies and products. Genuine original thinking does not cost a penny, and with a bit of it you can really leap ahead of the competition.

3. Don't take rejection personally

You are going to get a lot of knock-backs in business – the secret is not to let them get you down. As any nightclub Casanova will tell you – success is a numbers game.

4. Cash is king - hire a dragon

You haven't sold anything until the cash is in your bank. Lack of cash can bust even the brightest business. Hire a dragon to keep control of yours.

5. Cost your own time properly

Your business's scarcest resource? It's your time. Only spend it on the areas where you add the most value. Cost your own time properly – you might be willing to work for 50p an hour, but you won't find anyone else who will.

6. Be expensive

Raise your price until your customers squeak. Remember, the right price is what your customers are willing to pay. Your costs only tell you if you've got a good deal from your suppliers.

7. Get out of engine room and on to bridge

Don't spend weeks lovingly crafting an intricate business plan then dump it in a drawer. Take time out regularly to think about the direction of your business, even if your plans are scribbled on the back on an envelope.

8. Get a mentor

Starting in business can be like climbing a mountain in flip-flops with only a road map to guide you. Why not get the advice of someone who has been there before?

9. Be flexible

While determination is everything, you have to be prepared to make quick changes along the way. Fix on your destination, but be willing to change the route you take to get there.

10. Be persistent

Our greatest glory is not in never falling; it is in rising every time we fall. Surround yourself with supporters so you keep your mojo even when things are bad.

Preface to the second edition

When you start out in business, it's easy to feel like you are the smallest acorn, impossibly dwarfed in the shadows of the mighty business oaks around you. It's hard to remember that the largest companies in the world started from bedrooms, market stalls and backs of vans.

Business isn't rocket science, but too many guides treat it like it is. My aim with this book is to demonstrate how simple starting up and growing your business is. I want to pass on tips, nuggets of wisdom and inspiration from countless entrepreneurs young and old. I also want to show you how much fun and rewarding business can be.

One of the best additions to this edition is from the hundreds of emails I've had from readers, from Kent to Kazahkstan. I've included their experiences and advice in this book.

"I've read lots of manuals by boring old farts who left their sense of humour at the office door." (Carole)

I admit there were a couple of odd emails:

"I'm Keen to meet up litrally anytime like now!"

But in the main they were insightful and motivating. I've also included some new sections on your recommendations, such as 'hunting a mentor' and 'pitching'.

I've built the guidance in this book from my own experience. I have started and run a succession of businesses – such as an event organiser called 'Let me hold your balls for you', and a magazine I launched by living in a shop window for a week surviving just off the internet and my current custom publishing agency, Editions. When I talk about the importance of having a hangover to come up with good ideas or crying as a negotiating technique, I'm speaking from painful experience!

But I'm keenest to prove that entrepreneurship is open to anyone. As my best friend Paul kindly observed, 'The Caspian I grew up with couldn't spot a gap in the pavement, let alone a gap in the market'. Don't be put off by the born hustlers we see on our TVs. The real success stories are the millions of people who are quietly living their dreams around the country today.

I hope you enjoy the book and find it useful. I would very much like to know your feedback, hints and opinions so that I can share them with other budding entrepreneurs in the future.

You can email me at: **caspian@fromacorns.com**.

Good luck!

Caspian Woods

The *From Acorns* website

- The *From Acorns* website links in lots of practical tools and templates that are referenced in the book.
- There is also a collection of other articles and more detailed thoughts on topics.

Simply log on at **www.fromacorns.com**

How to make our country more successful

There is no doubt that countries with a wellspring of entrepreneurial talent bubbling out have a great advantage over the rest of the world. But there's one more thing they need – customers.

We are all a bit shy of taking a risk, but next time you see someone with a new and innovative product or service, you must make a vow to do one thing: *patronise them.*

I mean this of course in the old sense of the word. The best thing you can give a small business is your custom. So, take a risk. Give small businesses the chance to pitch for your work, and give them the benefit of the doubt. Be flexible in how you use them – and pay them early!

- It's great for them – they get growth.
- It's great for you – you get a highly motivated supplier.
- It's great for the country as a whole.

Acknowledgements

I'd fancifully imagined that writing a second edition was a matter of slapping some new quotes on the front cover and padding a chapter or two. Four months later, after a virtual re-write, I've learnt the hard way that you can be your own worst critic. So I'd like to thank the following for supporting me in my unforeseen labours.

My wife, Julie, for giving me the encouragement, honest feedback, and space while I bashed away. To Scarlett and Felix for their patience while I did 'boring work' rather than playing 'pouncing jagulars'.

At my 'day job', I'd like to salute our fantastic team at Editions. Ruth, Nan, Jane, Elizabeth, Chris, Alex, Aly, John, Stuart, Kate, Laura, Alan, Amy-Joy and Colin. It might be a cliché, but it's a joy and privilege to come in to work with you. Thanks also to our clients for giving us the creative freedom to do adventurous things.

The publishers at Pearson Education have long-championed the cause of entrepreneurship before it became so fashionable. My thanks to Samantha Jackson for being very tolerant while I misguidedly attempted to teach her to suck eggs, Natasha, Liz, Julie and Rachael Stock for gestating the first edition.

My greatest luck was being born the fifth child of a lively family. My thanks to father and mother, Patricia, Emma, Mark and Julie, Rupert and Pru and Adam and Megan, for allowing me to get away with murder, but sitting on me when I got too cocky. And Sam and Andy for admiring the 'jiggerly acorns'.

Finally to Paul Welham for the very amusing, but sadly unpublishable additions to the book and Alistair Rutherford for doing surprising things so I can write about them.

CHAPTER 1

Oaks from small acorns grow . . .

Oaks from small acorns grow . . .

Some years ago, a young entrepreneur called Marcus Samuel set up a small shop in the East End of London. He spotted a growing craze for seashells, partly for decoration, and partly for natural history enthusiasts. He set about specialising in this market.

After a while, and being an enterprising type of chap, he soon realised he could make more money from actually shipping the shells in from the Far East and selling them to other shops. The Marcus Samuel Shipping and Trading Company was born.

On a business trip there, his son spotted that there was also an abundance of oil which they could ship at the same time, and built a special boat for this. The year was 1890, and the company changed its name, in recognition of its main cargo, to the Shell Transport and Trading Company. As the demand for oil really took off and replaced the shells, the company became good old Shell Oil.

Shell is today the largest retailer in the world.

The moral of this story? Every business starts as an acorn. Yet when you are taking your first baby steps into business, it is far too easy to be daunted by the vast business oaks that seem to surround you.

Well, don't be. Take a look at a cross-section of the household names of today: Marks & Spencer, Monsoon, Microsoft, JP Morgan. They started from market stalls, bedrooms, barrows and backs of vans.

But the Shell story got me wondering. Why don't

more market stalls grow into multinationals? What's so special about the Marcus Samuel's of this world?

That's the aim of this book. By passing on the tips and advice of those who made it, hopefully it will give a helping hand to others. But most importantly it's about you – and instilling the belief and behaviours that will help you think and act like an habitual entrepreneur.

CHAPTER 2

What is it like?

What is it like?

Before you launch yourself headlong into your new business venture, it's important to know what you are letting yourself in for.

It is very tempting to look at the self-employed and think – 'Ah the lucky people, they don't have a boss, they can work whenever they want, they have flunkeys to do all the dirty work, and yet they get paid loads of money'.

There are certainly lots of benefits to being self-employed, and we'll come on to those. But first, let's be realistic about the costs.

The downside

Risk: Risk and reward go hand in hand in a new business. Most people just get hung up on the worry of financial risk.

> *A small business owner was fed up when his bank (to avoid litigation, let's call them High Street Bank) called in his overdraft. So he changed his name by deed poll to 'HighStreetbankarecapitalistbastards' and went to his branch where he demanded they write him out a cheque, in his new name, for the remaining funds in his account.*

However, the greatest fear you will have to overcome is the risk of being seen to fail, of 'friends' and competitors saying 'I told you so', and the possible dent to your self-esteem. If you want to know what failure is really like, turn to Chapter 24.

Hard work: Without doubt, running your business in the early days will be harder than working for someone else. Quite often your family, your friends and your social life will come a poor second to your new business. You have to be sure that this is the right time in your life to be making this type of commitment.

Responsibility: In your own business the buck stops with you. Unfortunately, it also has a tendency to follow you home at night. If you are the kind of person who lies in bed worrying at night about the government's exchange rate policy, or whether the neighbour's tree is encroaching on your garden, then think hard about the added worries that running your own business will bring you.

Timing is vital for small business success. If you are not sure this is the right moment for you, then don't worry. Keep your dreams bubbling away and your plans on ice until the right moment arrives to take the jump.

The upside

Of course, there are many benefits to running your own venture. Chief among these are:

Control over your own destiny: It is no coincidence that many entrepreneurs hate being told what to do. One of the major benefits of being self-employed is the chance to do things your own way, work your own hours, turn up to work in your pyjamas if the mood takes you. It sure beats working for someone you don't respect. Surprisingly, being self-employed can be a lot *less* stressful than working for someone else and, in this ever-changing world, sometimes offers more job security.

A chance to prove yourself:

> I was with a group of entrepreneurs who were speaking at a schools' careers convention. We were asked how well we had done at school. It turned out that, without exception, we were all underachievers, drop-outs, slackers or daydreamers. I still have the school report that says 'Caspian might achieve something if he woke up for five minutes and could remember where his books are'.

From meeting and interviewing many successful entrepreneurs, I have found that deep down they are often driven to prove themselves to others because of a strong feeling of personal inadequacy.

This typically stems from a formative stage in childhood. Many entrepreneurs, like Richard Branson, are dyslexics, some moved to foreign countries at a young age, one was moved from a very smart private school to the rough comprehensive next door when his father's business collapsed. Whatever the reasons, their endeavours certainly make the world a more interesting place. Business is a great way to prove everyone else wrong, and have the satisfaction of having built it all yourself.

A chance to create things: For many people, the greatest satisfaction is that of creating things from nothing or indulging in a passion. Getting paid to do this can almost seem like a wonderful bonus.

Money: We can't forget the moolah! It was certainly the view of the mechanic fixing my car last week. 'Money doesn't buy you happiness,' I opined lamely. 'Hmm,' said the mechanic, 'my neighbour won £3 million on the lottery and you couldn't have taken the smile off his face with a spanner.'

If you want to become seriously wealthy, then self-employment is probably the way to go. It is not so much that you can pay yourself whatever you want, it is the chance of perhaps selling out for millions. However, I have put money deliberately at the bottom of the list. This is where it comes in many interviews with successful entrepreneurs. Almost without fail, their advice is:

Follow your dreams first, and the money will come after

CHAPTER 3

What is an entrepreneur, and am I one?

What is an entrepreneur, and am I one?

When you read the word 'entrepreneur', what's the mental image that pops into your head?

I bet the great beardy Virgin king himself is in there somewhere. But who's that lurking behind? Yes, it's Del-Boy Trotter and his empire, Trotters Independent Trading! He was rebranding his tap water as 'Peckham Spring Water' long before Coca-Cola ever cottoned on to the wheeze.

When we think of entrepreneurs, we often think of born hustlers. They wouldn't just sell their grandmothers, they would lease them out on a time-share basis registered in Bermuda.

That's great, and many entrepreneurs are like this. But I'm not like that. And when I meet other entrepreneurs, I find many of them don't fit this image. In fact, give me almost any stereotype of an entrepreneur, and I'll show you the opposite.

- *'You must have come from a really poor background.'* That certainly doesn't apply to Charles Dunstone, who founded Carphone Warehouse – he went to a posh private school.
- *'You must be a macho, take-no-prisoners salesman.'* I don't think Anita Roddick, who founded The Body Shop, would agree with that.
- *'If you didn't start your first business before you were ten, then you're not an entrepreneur.'* Hold on. When Ray Krok founded McDonald's, he was into his sixties!

Do I have to be born an entrepreneur?

Thousands of hours of academic study and heated pub arguments have gone into answering this question.

To be sure, when you meet an archetypal entrepreneur it's hard to imagine them doing anything else. They were the ones who were told in primary school they would either end up in prison, or as a millionaire – and often end up doing both.

But beyond this minority of born hustlers, there is a huge variety of very successful entrepreneurs who certainly don't fit this mould. So, don't worry if you don't think you look the part, or you are allergic to sheepskin coats. If all you have is the enthusiasm to start something, and a willingness to take a bit of risk, then the world is yours for the taking.

> *"I know it's going to be OK because I recognise myself in many of the scenarios you describe." (Kate, social care)*

What type of entrepreneur am I?

There is no 'right' type of entrepreneur. Many people's goal is to have the financial freedom to do what they enjoy the most, and this can come from an income of £6,000 rather than £600,000. However, it's essential you know from the outset what type of entrepreneur you want to be, as this will affect many of your business decisions.

Lifestyle entrepreneur: You want to earn a good standard of living for yourself, and be in control of your destiny. However, you don't want lots of staff and responsibility. Many people use the term 'lifestyle entrepreneur' as a put-down. It's difficult to see why:

> *'John' is a graphic designer who specialises in whisky labels. His business consists of him, his old Volvo and his Labrador. However, he has an international reputation, he commands great fees for his work, he gets the satisfaction of seeing his work around the world, and can pick and choose when and where he works.*

If this sums up your approach, then bear in mind the following challenges you might face:

- Your most precious resource is your time. So although you are keen not to take on and manage staff, bear in mind that a few supporters can take a huge amount of non-productive work off your shoulders.
- Price your time accurately and learn to say no to the 'wrong' type of work.
- Isolation will be a risk for you. Make sure you have a good network of supporters.
- You will probably have fewer clients. Nurturing strong relationships with them is essential.

Empire builder: For you, big is definitely beautiful! You may not know what business this will be in, just so long as you can grow it. You think Citizen Kane is a good type of role model. Money is a feature of your dreams, but so is being applauded on to a podium by your peers.

- The most important challenge for you is your business sector. Make sure you are going into an industry with strong upward growth.
- Make sure someone is watching the cashflow, tax and legals, as you'll be too busy selling.
- Keep scheming. Your path to growth will often involve a few tactical shifts.
- Build a good team around you of people who are better at their jobs than you are, and learn to let go of the reins.

Social entrepreneur: You have probably never thought of yourself as an entrepreneur. You are certainly not doing it for the money. However, you have a strong desire to bring your vision to fruition, whether it is opening an art gallery, taking a group of disadvantaged youngsters to Disneyland, or changing a particularly unjust piece of legislation. One reader is working on a shampoo for patients with chemotherapy-induced hair loss. Another runs a marketing agency working to reduce children's deaths in cars, which in the UK is one of the highest in Europe.

You are just as much an entrepreneur as the others, and there is plenty in this book you can learn from.

The intrapreneur: You are someone who sets up a business under the wing of your current employer. You don't own all of the company, but have a degree of reward linked to performance.

> *Ajaz Ahmed joined Dixons as a shopfloor worker at 16 on £30 a week. He was determined to be rich. He bought a computer and was amazed no one could tell him how to connect to the internet. He pestered his bosses that they had to be the first company to help get their customers online, which eventually led to the foundation of Freeserve. The company grew and at one stage was worth more than Dixons itself. When it was sold for £1.6 billion, although a minority shareholder, Ajaz made a good deal of money.*

As one reader, Greg, recounted:

> *"When my company sold out to a larger company, it was very depressing and I decided to start my own business and bought this book for inspiration. It helped me so much with my attitude and business reasoning that in little time I spotted an area in which the new company could turn around an extra £300k. They have since offered me a European product manager's position, to look at other obvious areas. I am still going to start my own business in the near future, but its refreshing to know that you can be employed and still be a good business person."*

Remember, there is no one definition of who an entrepreneur is. What will distinguish you as an entrepreneur is not who you *are*, but what you *do*. It's about actions and behaviours. To quote the multimillionaire, Sir Tom Hunter:

> *It's not IQ that matters, it's I CAN!*

And the best thing about this? While we might not have been born entrepreneurs, we can learn to act like one. Let's see how.

CHAPTER 4

How to become an entrepreneur

How to become an entrepreneur

According to my *Collins English Dictionary*, the word 'entrepreneur' derives from a nineteenth-century French word meaning 'to undertake'. The exact definition is:

> *The owner of an enterprise who, by risk and initiative, attempts to make profits.*

If you want to become more entrepreneurial, then you have to work on those two behaviours:

- risk
- initiative.

Make yourself a bigger risk-taker

I confess to dropping out of an economics degree. However, there was one fundamental economic equation that stuck in my head in between bouts of snoozing:

 Profit is the reward for risk

To be successful you have to be prepared to take a risk.

The most obvious risk people think of is the financial one. But there is a bigger risk that people don't often admit to. It's the fear of standing out from the crowd. It's the fear of being judged by those around us. It's not actually the fear of failure – it's the fear of being *seen* to fail by your colleagues, your family, your friends, your neighbours. It is a fear of looking stupid, or of people saying, 'I told you so'. It is a fear, ultimately, of rejection. This fear is the greatest barrier to entrepreneurship in Britain.

My first entrepreneurial venture was to produce a yearbook for my final year at university. It was pretty irreverent, with lots of compromising photos, a few rude words and lists of who everyone most wanted to snog. I invested about £1,000 I didn't have to print the books.

Along came graduation day. I set up a stall and stood there, smiling nervously, waiting to see if anyone would actually buy one. Instead, the first person to appear was an ancient cobweb covered academic who shuffled out of nowhere like Herman Munster. He picked up the yearbook and thumbed through it while I watched nervously to see my first customer's reaction. He tossed it back on the desk and said, 'What complete rubbish. It is a disgrace to the university name, and I'm going to have it stopped immediately.' He turned around and lumbered off.

I never heard from or saw him again. The students piled in, and they bought (or more accurately, got their parents to buy) lots of the yearbooks, and I earned enough to pay the printers and get my first business off the ground.

But at the time, I was bricking it. His comments really struck home, and many years later I can still remember the fear I felt at the time.

Unfortunately, this isn't just the one-time risk of walking in and telling the boss where to shove his job. You have to become a perpetual risk-taker in your business.

- You have to take a risk in making your product/service stand out from the crowd.
- You have to take a risk with your marketing and promotion to have a chance of cutting through the noise.
- You have to face the personal rejection inevitable in selling your idea.

But you can learn to be better at this. Entrepreneurship is a matter of behaviour, and behaviours are something we can change. Just as we can get over a fear of heights or public speaking, so we can learn to be better risk-takers. Psychologists estimate it takes between 7 to 21 days to form a new habit or behaviour, so why not try some of the following exercises to help?

Exercise One: Kill your McTaggarts

I was doing some marketing consultancy for the founder of a successful computer company. He was a guy you could listen to all night. He was passionate and full of great tales about the early days of computing, sharing beers with Bill Gates, and setting up early satellite systems. But when we looked at his company's image and marketing, it was tired, dull and run of the mill.

I asked him, 'Why don't you put more of your passion and originality into your business?' He replied, 'Well, we have a client called [for the sake of argument] McTaggarts of Dundee. They are a family-run firm and have been around for generations. We have to be serious for them and present in suits and ties or they won't use us.'

So, they let the McTaggarts of Dundee dictate the agenda for the other 99 per cent of their customer base, and hamper their growth.

The problem is, we all have these McTaggarts.

They might be clients who have criticised us, friends who secretly resent us for being more successful than they are, parents who don't want us to get hurt, teachers at school who were blinkered, spouses worried about the mortgage.

The other problem is that we listen to them and accept their limitations. They stop us thinking and acting passionately and effectively. They stop us being different and creative, and entrepreneurial. So, we must kill them. OK, not literally, but through the following steps.

Toolkit: **Silence your critics by using this exercise and the steps below.**

The McTaggart	Situation	My assumed reason	Evidence?	Real reason
Example: *Head of marketing at blue chip firm*	*I made a cold call, and he was rude to me*	*I felt our products were too poor to interest him*	*✗*	*He gets 30 cold calls a day and is extremely busy*

- *Column 1:* You need to draw up a list of who your possible McTaggarts are. You might know some instantly. To work out the others, try asking the following questions:
  - Who laughed at an idea of mine, or advised me not to do something I really wanted to do?
  - What pieces of criticism can I remember recently, and who did they come from?
  - If I were on stage delivering a speech and I forgot my words, who would I hate most to see in that audience?
  - Who would I be most embarrassed about admitting my wildest ambitions to?
- *Column 2:* For each person, describe the particular situation or criticism.
- *Column 3:* At the time, what did you assume was the reason for them making this judgement?
- *Column 4:* Just a simple tick or cross: did they explicitly give you this reason, or did you just assume it?
- *Column 5:* What else might have been going on in their lives, situation or personality that would have led to the criticism, other than your behaviour?

The exercise should help with the following:
- You will start to realise who the real negatives and inhibitors are in your life.
- Even if you end up with 20 or more on your list (and I bet you don't), they will still only account for 1 per cent of your possible audience.
- In many cases, we have never asked them! We have assumed the reason for their criticism and blamed ourselves.
- They have a completely different agenda that might explain their actions and comments. The more personal the criticism, the more likely that this is fuelled by their jealousy, embarrassment, or frustration than any fault of yours.
- And in the few rare cases where the criticism might be justified, who cares? We can't all be perfect machines, and a personal weakness is often just the mirror image of another real strength you have.

Exercise Two: Confront your fears

Entrepreneurs don't become brave overnight. They do it little bit by little bit. I've also noticed that many of the most successful had very powerful mothers nurturing their enterprising behaviours.

> *Richard Branson's mother used to drive him into the country-side and give him a challenge to find his own way home (if you have hyperactive kids, I know how tempting the thought might be, but I do think she gave him some guidance!)*
>
> *The mother of Bill Cullen, one of Ireland's foremost entre-preneurs, used to send him to the shop to buy things. Then she would make him take one item back and haggle with the shop-keeper to give him his money back.*

By gradually confronting your fears you find they are only powerful because they are nurtured and fed in a dark corner of your imagination.

> *When I was eight, I got a part in the school play,* Murder in the Cathedral *by T.S. Eliot. It was so heavy we never got round to rehearsing the last scene. The first performance took place in front of every pupil in the school. The problem was – I hadn't learnt my lines. 'No problem', I thought, 'nor has anyone else, and someone is bound to fluff before it gets to me.'*
>
> *Only they didn't.*
>
> *So I found myself standing on stage with 200 of my peers staring at me, and not a clue what to say. The short-tempered drama teacher prompted me ... I still didn't know ... he prompted again ... silence. In front of the whole school, he walked on stage, shouted at me, hauled me off stage by my ear and cancelled the performance.*
>
> *So today, do I break into a cold sweat if I have to present to an audience? Not in the slightest. It was such a traumatic event that presenting to anyone since that day has been a complete walk in the park compared to that!*

The RAF parachute school has a great motto:

Knowledge dispels fear

To teach sensible people to jump out of a perfectly serviceable plane they practise again and again and again. They make you jump off benches, then off walls, then off scaffolding. By the time you come to jumping out of a plane, you are so fed up with all the training, you practically throw yourself out in frustration.

So, take the same approach.

- Write down a list of your worst possible fears in business.
- Try to find a small way to confront these in bite-sized chunks. If it's selling, start off with a list of 'easy' calls to make. If it's public speaking, find a local club or school where you can give a speech and don't worry if it goes wrong. Then gradually build up to bigger challenges from there.

You will soon find the things that petrify you most now are never as bad in reality.

Some common fears people have in business: Throughout this book, we look at overcoming barriers and fears. However, you might be too nervous to take the plunge because of one specific fear. If so, take a look at these sections first, and how to overcome your fears, and then get into the rest of the book:

Starting a business that might fail:	Learn to love failure: see page 192.
Cold-calling and selling to strangers:	Prepare yourself for rejection: see page 117.
Running out of money:	Cash is king: see page 148.
Raising money:	What does a funder look for?: see page 70.

Exercise Three: Become an immigrant

It is no coincidence that many successful entrepreneurs through history were immigrants. The reason? They have no emotional baggage in their new country. They can break all the rules, make lots of mistakes and not have to worry about their neighbours looking over the fence saying, 'Couldn't he get a proper job?'

If you can't physically set yourself up in a different town, there are some ways to become a 'virtual immigrant' even in your own house:

> Steve Jobs was brought back into Apple Computers to help turn the company around. He was worried that the prevailing mindset didn't encourage innovation. So he set up a unit called 'SkunkWorks'. They were in a different building, they didn't mix with the other staff or talk to them. They even flew a pirate flag from their roof. This team came up with the iPod.

Similarly, don't tell your family and friends about your plans. If you want to talk it through, do it with complete strangers whose opinions you don't care about.

CHAPTER 5

What's your motivation?

What's your motivation?

The second part of the definition of an entrepreneur was 'initiative'. Other words for this might be drive, motivation, ambition. If risk is the brakes on your engine, initiative is the fuel that fires your business forwards.

> *Mark Mills wondered why only the Royal Mail was allowed to have postboxes. There could be a business there for him. So he phoned them up and asked. They laughed at him saying, 'We get hundreds of people asking this, and it's our sole right by law'.*
>
> *But Mark's curiosity was piqued. He enrolled in law school at nights. He spent time looking at the law. What he discovered was that Royal Mail only had a monopoly on supplying the locks to postboxes. Anyone could in fact supply the boxes.*
>
> *Mark quickly sited loads of postboxes in petrol stations round the country. The Royal Mail supplied the locks. He then sold advertising space on these to a multinational oil company, and then sold his business.*

What distinguished Mark was that he took action, and didn't give up like the hundreds of others.

It is this drive and motivation that marks out successful entrepreneurs.

The five-second multimillionaire test

A famous Hollywood actor would use this test to see if aspiring actors had what it took to become famous. He would simply ask them:

Do you want to be an actor, or must you be an actor?

He would then measure how long their answer took. If they paused for a second, he told them they wouldn't make it.

You can ask yourself the same question:

(a) Would you like to be successful? Do you like the idea of not having to answer to a boss, of having creative control, having a smart car and great holidays?

Or:

(b) Must *you be successful, no matter what?*

While you can be successful if you answered (a), I would say the degree of hesitation you have over that answer will predict the scale of your success.

The richest man in Britain at the moment, Roman Abramovich, was born in poverty in the Arctic Circle and was orphaned at the age of four. You probably don't have to wonder about what drives him. Compare this to the motivation the following reader gave:

"I left a 14-year career in a big company two weeks ago – senior role, well paid – and my plan is to start up something completely different from scratch after a break. I've always fancied the idea of working for myself and finally admitted that I couldn't stand the politics, couldn't conform as much as clearly was required and didn't like being told what to do, so I've taken the plunge."

That point made, we don't all have to strive to be mega-millionaires. I can tell you that only being moderately successful as an entrepreneur is extremely rewarding. And, as they say, 'Unhappy is the land that needs heroes'.

The following can help build your motivation.

Polish your dreams

When mountaineers get out of their tent in the morning, what is the first thing they do? They look up at the summit of the mountain. If all they thought about was the long slow slog in front of them each day, they would never leave their tent. They keep going because they are dreaming of the summit.

It's the same in business. If you are clearly focused on your summit, then the broken rocks you have to clamber over on your daily path will just become an annoyance. If you've lost sight of your summit, all you'll ever notice is the hard daily slog.

We all have fantastic dreams as children: becoming a racing driver, millionaire, brain surgeon. It's just that along the way, we let go of them.

I'll let you in on a little secret of very successful entrepreneurs:

The people who achieve their dreams are the people who hold on to them

A young boy called Jim McColl had a dream to have a chauffeur-driven Bentley. He is now a successful businessman and recently personally netted £100 million from selling an offshoot of his main company Clyde Blowers. I walked with him out of an event once. Guess what was waiting for him outside?

The two worst things we can do with our dreams is 'rationalise' them and make them 'realistic'. If they were realistic, they wouldn't be dreams in the first place!

Here are some tips for better dreaming:

- Don't let other people rationalise your ambitions. I remember a teacher asking me what I wanted to become when I was older. I said an international publishing mogul. My, how they laughed. If you're going to tell someone your wildest dreams, tell a complete stranger. Don't share it with the McTaggarts. They will say 'Yes, but ...' Little by little, this will erode your dream until there is nothing left.
- Stop worrying in detail about how you are going to get there. Start off with where you want to end up, and then work backwards from there. Think, 'If I'm going to be a Hollywood director, I'd better start to muck about with a camcorder' rather than 'I'll never make it to Hollywood from Norwich. I'd better settle on doing local wedding videos.'

- It is *never* too late. Remember: Ray Krok started MacDonald's in his sixties!
- It is OK to start off with a vague dream. But it only becomes a powerful incentive the more you polish it. Add more details to your goal, and really start to visualise it. Think of the fine details, or what a typical day in your dream life will be like. Some people I know actually carry around photographs of what they want.
- Read inspirational books. I've included a few on page 207.

CHAPTER 6

Some very useful skills

Some very useful skills

You are the key to the success of your business. Your personal strengths and weaknesses will quickly become magnified in your business. However, before you subject yourself to too much grief, remember:

 No one is perfect

> *An artist did a project with the staff of a major company. He asked them to draw an image that best represented their chief executive. They drew a picture of a large loose cannon careering down the hill with a tiny short fuse. It made an enormous noise when it went off, but released a tiny cannon ball that only rolled three feet.*

We all have weaknesses. In fact, the most nervous public speaker I have ever heard is Richard Branson. Usually the weaknesses are just the flip sides of our greatest strengths. The most important thing is that you do an honest appraisal of yourself to find what your strengths and weaknesses are so that you can compensate for them.

Coming up with an honest assessment of yourself can be very hard to do. Try to be as honest and objective with yourself as possible. Don't be modest about your strengths, or overly critical with yourself. Think about what you enjoy doing most, and what aspects of work you don't like – these will usually correspond with your strengths and weaknesses.

Toolkit: **To help you find out what your skills and gaps are, complete the following exercise.**

If it makes it easier, ask a trusted and impartial friend to help you with this.

Strengths	
What are your advantages?	
What types of tasks do you most enjoy doing?	
What do you do well?	
What specific skills and experience do you have which might help you?	
Weaknesses	
What could you improve?	
What types of jobs do you dislike most?	
What should you avoid doing?	
Are there areas of technical knowledge or experience that you are weak in?	

Assertiveness

Being assertive is a hard thing to do well. It is not about becoming a tyrant. It is about having a deep-seated belief in your own worth.

Confidence: This is the magic elixir in success. It is hard to quantify, and yet governs the economies of the world. Fundamentally, it is a belief that you have something unique to offer.

In fact, confidence is a fluid thing. It is not something we are born with, but something that gets built up over time from positive feedback we receive. It is vital you keep your self-belief constantly topped up. See Chapter 25 'Mojo medicine' for tips on how to do this.

Don't undersell yourself: While a lack of confidence provides a very strong drive to prove yourself, it can cause you problems. You might undersell yourself, charge too low a price for your work, give in at negotiations, over-promise to your customers, or get taken for a ride by suppliers.

Learn to say 'no': Success is about focus. Often you will find yourself having politely to say 'no' to potential customers, suppliers or friends in order to have time left for the good stuff. It is also vital to get into the habit of telling customers when you can't do something.

> **♟ Entrepreneur's Secret: Under-promise/over-deliver**
> If you give your client a rash promise on a delivery time and miss it by a day, your client will be far more angry than if you'd told them upfront how long the job would realistically take.

I would recommend going on an assertiveness course. I know it sounds embarrassing – I did one when I started up and a friend and I just sat giggling at the back of the class. However, it soon dawned on me that this was important stuff, and what I learnt keeps cropping up throughout my life.

Time management

I love deadlines. I especially like the whooshing sound they make as they go flying by. (Douglas Adams)

While being busy makes you feel important, you must learn to delegate non-essential tasks

Doesn't time management sound a bit trivial? Well, time is the stuff life is made of.

When you start out you will typically dash around doing everything from ordering stationery to scrubbing dishes. That's fine for a start (and cheap!) and gives you a good feeling for how everything works.

However, you will find that you spend only 20 per cent of your time doing the stuff that adds 80 per cent of the value to your business. Unless you work out what is essential to your business and what jobs just get in the way (or could be done better by someone else) you will be stuck doing the same thing in ten years' time. If you want to grow to a million-pound business, you can't spend all day licking envelopes.

Toolkit: **On the website there is a simple timesheet template (www.fromacorns.com). Try it with the following tips.**

- Go on a time-management course. It might cost you a few quid, but it is one of the best single investments you can make. Pick up the phone now and book yourself a course. Go on, now – I mean it!
- If your work involves computers, delete all the games off your machine – *now!* Microsoft Solitaire is a sinister plot to destroy western productivity.
- Give yourself an easy task to start the day. My dad has a good theory: when he is writing he always leaves the last paragraph of his day unfinished. The next morning, he therefore has an easy way to start working again.
- Avoid interruptions – friends, the post and emails. Try to schedule a set time of day for these.
- Work out your most creative time of day. Do the most important or hard things then.
- Give yourself a break. You are not a robot – give yourself a reward once you have done your tasks. Go out for some fresh air.
- Cut yourself some slack. When planning a project, always put a week at the end for some imaginary task. You will always need it.
- Learn to realise that just because a task is urgent, it doesn't mean it's important. By thinking and acting long term you can save a lot of crises.

The ability to listen

Your aim is not to shift products. Your aim is to satisfy your customers' needs

This is the heart of selling. The most important skill is being able to find out *exactly* what your customers' needs are. This isn't as easy as it sounds.

Sometimes, your customers won't actually know what it is they want.

> *"I think the word 'innovative' should be banned. We're often asked for this by clients, but then they reject our ideas as 'no-one has done it before'!" (Mark, engineer)*

Or if the customers know, they won't tell you. Think of the times you're having a lousy meal in a restaurant when the waiter asks you 'Is everything OK?'. 'Oh, fine thanks!' you reply brightly, vowing under your breath never to return.

Opportunity sometimes knocks very quietly. You need to learn to be a listener. You also need to learn how to ask the right questions and read what your customers' hidden needs and wants might be.

For a dyed-in-the-wool entrepreneur, this can be tricky, as you actually need to learn when to shut up!

See Chapter 16 for more information on the art of selling.

CHAPTER 7

Your million-pound business idea

Your million-pound business idea

If you want to get rich, you need to do three things: get up early, work hard and strike oil. (John Paul Getty, Texan oil billionaire)

 A rising tide lifts all boats

It's pretty easy to double the size of your business every year if the industry you are in is growing by 200 per cent per year. You will be amazed at how very intelligent people have quite small businesses, or those running multinationals seem, well, not the sharpest knives in the cutlery drawer.

Alex Tew was about to go to university but was worried he wouldn't have enough money. He says he went to bed that night worrying about the problem, and woke up in the morning with the idea of the 'Million Dollar Home Page'. A page on the internet is made up of about 1 million pixels. He decided to sell each one to advertisers for a dollar each. The genius of the idea was its simplicity, and the fact it generated hype. It was picked up by media sources round the world. As Alex said, 'As I made money, more people talked about it and the more people talked about it, the more money I made'. The wall-to-wall coverage led to a flood of visitors to his site, and – in their trail – many eager advertisers. Within four months, his page was full, and his million made.

There might be a good reason why no one has thought of your 'brilliant idea' before

I've since received a few emails from people wanting to follow in Alex's footsteps and set up similar sounding sites and asking for advice. Too late. There's no prize for being second with an idea like that.

So, it's worth spending a bit of time thinking through the growth potential of your idea. Even if you think you have a good idea, it is still worth seeing if there is a spin you can put on it to make it more unique.

Eleven ways to come up with a brilliant business idea

1. **It doesn't have to be your own**: It is a myth that all entrepreneurs are good at generating brilliant ideas. No – they are brilliant at making things happen. Don't be too proud to look to other people and their businesses for inspiration. If you are a natural sales person, perhaps consider teaming up with a boffin who has a cracking idea.

   One of Richard Branson's most successful businesses is his airline, but it wasn't his idea. Someone else approached him with the plans in place. Richard's genius was in making it happen.

2. **Think laterally**: Cast your net widely when looking for new ideas. Look overseas for ideas – some of the best businesses have been imported from other countries. Sir Tom Farmer's Kwik-Fit business came from a holiday he took to the USA. Read books on the subject, read research reports on future demographic trends. Two great websites for this are **www.trendwatching.com** and **www.springwise.com**. Similarly, you could import an idea that works well from a different industry.

3. **Look for change**: Periods of change are where lots of money can be made. This could be when there is new legislation coming to an industry, changes in customer-buying habits, the opening up of an industry, or new technology.

> *The revolutionary concept that nobody has thought of before is for your ego, not your wallet. Spot the trends and then follow the yellow brick road. (Duncan Bannantyne)*

While I think Duncan underestimates the power of innovative ideas, he certainly knows how to spot trends. He made his first £30 million by following Margaret Thatcher's decision to pay private businesses to look after the elderly. He sold his house, car, TV and maxed three credit cards to the limit to buy his first care home. His current business, Bannantyne's Health Clubs, has cashed in on the growth in fitness and is now valued at over £100 million.

4. **Listen very carefully to your customers**: Sometimes, all it takes is a single throw away line to alert an entrepreneur to a multimillion-pound business. The 'Dummies' series of guides came from a single customer someone overheard in a book-shop who said, 'I wish there was a simple computer guide for dummies like me ...'. There are now 125 million copies in print.

> *"I was listening to a local customer who was raving about how you couldn't get my services anywhere else, which made me realise I could specialise and expand beyond my local market." (Gillian, period costumes for museums)*

5. **Don't mistake a hearse for a bandwagon – be ahead of the game**: This is a very good comment from my publisher, Richard Stagg. If you can see a bandwagon, the chances are it has already left the station. If you are going into a popular industry, try to ensure you are on the next coming wave.

> *"I'm looking to start up as a web designer. Should I not bother?" (Angie, web business)*

When I got that email, I felt awful, as the last thing I want to do is put people off starting up. In my defence, I'll give you two newspaper stories from the same week I received that email:

- *Company A*: A web design company we use went into liquidation. When they started up, they had fantastic growth and lots of external finance. However, they said now there were too many cheap competitors for them to survive.
- *Company B*: Another local entrepreneur has just sold his web search optimisation company. Set up around the same time as company A, he saw that web search would be the next big trend, so was ahead of the game. He sold it for £50 million.

6. **Dominate a niche – be a Porsche, not a Ford**: Surely everyone wants to be Ford – the biggest car company in the world? Not when you think that Porsche is the most *profitable* car company in the world at the moment. Rather than trying to be all things to all people, try to look for a smaller specialist niche.

> *A typing business was struggling against a mountain of competition. So instead they decided to specialise in typing for engineers. All of sudden, they were in a market of one. They could charge more, they had fewer competitors and word of their specialist service spread rapidly to bring them new customers.*

This approach sounds so obvious to me that I'm bewildered not more people are doing it. I think it's the following hurdles that put them off:

- Many are worried about turning away customers who don't fit the niche. Look to the long term. You'll soon replace these 'run-of-the-mill' customers with more of your specialised ones, who'll pay more.
- Is it too much of a risk to specialise on one customer group? It does expose you to a downturn of work in that sector. I say, far better to ride the storm, and come out a better business, than always settle for mediocrity.
- The final worry is that of conflict – that you are working for competitors. Generally, so long as you are upfront about it, and have good confidentiality systems, customers are willing to trade the risk for your specialist knowledge and experience.

7. **Where there's mystery, there's margin**: A variation on the 'niche' approach is this advice from an irreverent IT entrepreneur, Mark Vickers. He told me how he would move his businesses into increasingly complex IT markets as soon as his current market became common knowledge. His profits came from making this complexity very simple for his customers.

8. **Start with what you know**: Everyone else's businesses look easy from the outside. Unfortunately, the odds of you coming up with a new idea that people love and no one has thought of before in an industry you know nothing about are slim – to say the least. While it's always good to approach a market with enthusiasm and a fresh eye, it's worth running your ideas past an industry veteran.

9. **Don't just go for a business you 'like'**: Countless people decide to run a restaurant because they like eating out, or set up a magazine because they like reading them. The quickest way to ruin a hobby is to make it your life. However, great satisfaction can come from running a successful business in many less 'glamorous' sectors – and ones often overlooked by the glory seekers!

10. **A gap in the market, but is there a market in the gap?** It is easy to get carried away about the importance of spotting a gap no one else is serving. You have to be very sure there is enough money in this gap.

A recent dot.com company cornered the market for delivering goods in 60 minutes. They had seen this done in America, and they were the first to do it in the UK. The problem was the market in the gap. They were often delivering things like aspirins and condoms worth £2, when delivery alone cost £2.50.

11. **Competition can be a good thing**: A common mistake is to look for a business with no competition. There might be a very good reason why this is so. It can be much better to enter a busy business sector, but do something strikingly innovative.

How to come up with creative ideas

Start from a different place: Sometimes you can be too close to a business to see the obvious.

NASA invested millions of dollars trying to design a pen that would work properly in space where there is no gravity to push the ink down the tube. The Russians used a pencil.

Our brains are fundamentally lazy and will continually try to make the obvious conclusions. The trick is to try to surprise your brain into doing something new.

There is nothing that is a more certain sign of insanity than to do the same thing over and over and expect the results to be different. (Albert Einstein)

Here are some ways to do this:
- Start by thinking of opposites – think of the worst things you could do for your customer.
- Don't be put off with ideas that make you laugh. Laughter is often a defence mechanism for the brain when faced with something new and challenging. The 'laugh-out-loud' idea is often a genuinely exciting opportunity in disguise (which is why it's sometimes not a good idea to discuss your fledgling idea with close friends or family!).

- Change your routine. Deliberately take a different route to work, and look around. For some reason, I get my best ideas when I have a hangover, and jot them into a little black 'hangover book'.
- Start with the problem. Our brains like to think in nice linear ways. So, when trying to get from point A to point C, they get continually stuck at B. Sometimes, like the Russian pencil, it's better to start at C and work backwards.

Don't knock it – hangovers can be a great source of business ideas

Two US venture capitalists are currently offering $2 million to anybody who can invent a cell phone battery that lasts five times as long as current ones.

Share your ideas: Remember the kids in school exams who would put their arms round their papers so no one would copy them? Don't become like them. For sure, don't go and tell your nearest competitors all your creative ideas, but by the same token, don't think just by jealously guarding your secret formula it'll work. Success is often more about perspiration and timing than just a simple idea.

Brainstorm your idea frequently with those around you. Sometimes, just explaining it to someone will make it much clearer in your own mind. If you're stuck, why not offer a small prize like a bottle of wine for the person who comes up with the best solution or name?

But bear in mind, sometimes it's easier to discuss ideas with relative strangers who have no preconceptions and won't prejudge you.

CHAPTER 8

Turning your idea into a business plan

Turning your idea into a business plan

If you don't know where you are going, it doesn't matter which road you take to get there. (Lewis Carroll, Alice's Adventures in Wonderland*)*

One of your first tasks will be to write a business plan. There are hundreds of books, training courses, software programs, websites and guides devoted to them.

But before throwing yourself headlong into this process, there are three basic rules you should apply.

Three rules of business plans

1. Who are you writing it for?

The most important audience for your plan is *yourself*. This is the one opportunity for you to think through all the implications of your business, and really check the assumptions you are making. For this reason, there is no simple template you must follow. It is also vital that this is your plan. There is no point paying an accountant to write the plan when you are going to be running the business.

The second most important audience is a potential funder. At this stage, your plan becomes a sales tool to raise you the finance. This often requires a different version of the plan.

2. Avoid paralysis by analysis

"The more I keep thinking my business idea over in my head, the shakier it looks." (Angela)

If you spend too long on a business plan, you will get bogged down in unimportant details. I've seen a business plan for a café where they had worked the costs out down to the last teaspoon.

I think this obsession with detail is underpinned by a psychological desire to make business seem like a predictable science, rather than the inexact human endeavour it actually is.

As a rule of thumb, when you find yourself classifying headlines with different colour codes – step away from the plan! Instead, let your mantra be that of Texan billionaire Ross Perot:

When I see a snake – I kill it. I don't appoint a committee on snakes.

3. Keep planning

As von Clausewitz, a Prussian general, said:

No plan survives the first contact with the enemy [or your customers in this case].

Almost as soon as your plan is written, it will be out of date. However, the most successful businesses are those that are continually adapting to changes in customers and the market. It is vital that your plan, once written, isn't consigned to the bottom drawer or the file marked 'dustbin'. Look at Chapter 23 for advice on strategy.

What does a funder look for in your business plan?

Where too many business plans are filed

Most people produce a business plan mainly to raise money. I have sat on many funding panels, and spoken to many bank managers, and it is useful to bear in mind the thought process a funder will go through when you sit in front of them:

1. Do I think *you* have what it takes to make this work (usually decided within 120 seconds of you walking through the front door)?

2. Does the overall business concept excite me (4 minutes)?

3. Can you reassure me that I will ever see my money again (the remaining 40 minutes or so)?

`00:00` OK, so the clock's running, let's see how you get on:

`02:00` **You:** Whether you are asking for £5, £5,000 or £500,000, the following is always true:

 Funders back people

No matter what your idea, funders are ultimately betting on your ability to make things happen. So how can you prove this?

- It's unfair, but first impressions *do* count. An experienced interviewer from a leading company once told me she usually decided on a candidate 40 seconds after they had walked in the door. So, look after the simple things. Dress smart, look people in the eye when you walk in, smile and shake hands. It makes a difference.
- Put details of any relevant experience in your plan. This could be work experience in your industry, or, better, examples of previous businesses you have run, or examples of your own initiative. (You organised a fashion show at school? Put it in.)
- Put in an analysis of your strengths and weaknesses. Don't make out you are superhuman – what they are looking for is an honest appreciation of your strengths and what you will do to balance your weaknesses.
- The most important thing is gumption, or staying power. Success will ultimately depend on your ability to keep going through tough times. Try to put examples of your drive and determination in your plan. Funders will also want to know you have thought things through. Be prepared to answer a whole range of 'what if' questions from your funders.

`06:00` **Excite me:** This is where you get people hooked with your sexy idea. The secret here is to keep it simple: outline the concept and summarise the main points. The plan should briefly look at your competitive position and, this is the clincher, *why your idea is different*. It is going to be hard to excite someone about backing another window cleaning business, but what's this? You are a former climber, and are the only person in Leeds who specialises in tall office buildings? Now I'm interested. Now all you have to do is ...

Reassure me: This is where we get to making sure your figures stack up.

> `46:00`

Financial forecasts

If you look at any business plan books you are likely to be daunted by the financials you are required to produce: balance sheets, P&L, three-year discounted cashflow, return on capital invested, binomial quadratic distribution, warp drive integer derivative ...

Let's stick to the basics.

Your revenue

This is the total amount of cash you receive. This typically depends on two things: the price you sell things for, and the number you can sell (I told you we were going to keep it basic).

Price: Price should not be determined by the cost of your product. Your price is what your customers are willing to pay and, as you might have seen with things like iced-mocha-cappuccinos, this can bear little relation to the cost. Price is a marketing issue – look at Chapter 14.

However, you have to know your break-even price – the *minimum* price you have to charge for each item to cover costs. We come on to this in a moment.

The number you sell: This is determined by two things: how big the market is and how many you can physically make and sell in a day. To determine the size of the market, you need to do some market research. This needs looking at in detail, as getting this wrong can have a serious impact on your business.

How to forecast your sales

> **Use research like a drunk uses a lamp-post – more for support than illumination**

Accurate market research is a notoriously tricky business – just look at election forecasts.

The dot.com boom and bust era was largely based on faulty market research, and much of it still goes on. This is what I call:

Waynestock Syndrome:

In Wayne's World 2, they are planning to hold a rock concert – Waynestock. They are worried about how many people will come until Jim Morrison appears in Wayne's dream and says: 'Hold it, and they will come'.

To follow the Waynestock method for your business, do a variation on the following:

1. You are selling Amazonian fighting fish. You do some research on the internet to find the total size of your likely target market. This could be, say, the total number of houses with ponds in the Manchester area, or the number of people in the UK last year who bought goldfish.
2. Make a modest assumption that, say, 1 per cent of this market should be yours in the first year, going up to 5 per cent, then 10 per cent in the following years. This will give you a first year revenue of £300,000. Sounds good!
3. ... er, that's it.

The problem with this approach, as you will have doubtless spotted, is that while the figures will seem modest, you have absolutely *no evidence* that people will buy one fish from you, let alone 10,000 of them. This is the problem with making assumptions.

If you ASSUME you make an ASS of U and ME. (Silence of the Lambs)

The only reliable way to make predictions (and the only ones your potential funders will believe) is to base them on experience.

Real-world sales forecasts: In an ideal world, you will have already tried selling some products before doing your business plan. By analysing these sales (How long did it take to get each customer? Do they fit in a distinct category like 'retired hobbyists'? Did they just buy from you because they were friends?) you can then realistically extend your forecasts.

Alternatively, you might have worked for an employer in this industry. Their figures should give you some indication. Again, make sure there are no underlying things you are missing out – i.e. it took them six years to build up to their current customer base, or their biggest customer also happens to be a relative (I know one large company where this was the case).

You might have a wise mentor who has been and done this all before and can tell you just what to do (see page 187 about hunting and capturing one of these mythical beasts).

Find out how your competitors are doing. You can apply various covert techniques, but by far the most effective I have found is just to phone them up and ask them point blank. You'll be amazed at how much they will tell you. People love to brag about themselves, and will often not see humble little you as a competitor. Again, put these figures through a reality filter. Are they deliberately underestimating to put you off? Does the bulk of their sales come from one customer they are not going to tell you about? Perhaps try to verify those stories from their staff or competitors.

You can also do your own research. This is not always as accurate as you might think.

Before producing my first university yearbook, I did a survey into what students would want to see in it, the ideal price, and whether they would buy one. I then produced the book on these assumptions. However, I discovered that telling someone you will pay £10 is very different from actually having to hand over £10 that could be spent on beer. I also found the real customers were their parents, and they would pay double that.

Beware of just researching among friends. If someone (particularly a friend) asked what you thought of their lovingly crafted porcelain angels, would you, (a) be callous, point out what dross they are and tell them they should never give up the day job, or, (b) smile sweetly, nod and back gently away?

> **♟Entrepreneur's Secret: Funders love 'letters of intent'**
> Providing a sheaf of letters confirming that 'Yes, David, I will definitely be ordering ten Amazonian fighting fish the moment they clear customs' is very impressive (but don't think they won't notice if they all have suspiciously similar handwriting . . .).

Your costs

Having worked out your revenue, you then need to calculate costs. There are two types of cost:

- your direct costs
- your overhead costs.

1. Direct costs

This is the cost of producing each item. It is made up of two elements:

- Raw material cost: This is the cost of the 'ingredients' in each product. Some of these will be obvious, but also look at hidden costs. If you are making pottery, don't just put in the cost of the clay; also estimate an element of the electricity or gas used to fire the item.
- The cost of your time: One of the biggest oversights people make starting out in business is failing to:

 Make sure you cost your own time properly

I'll illustrate. You want to sell your product for £5. The raw materials cost about 60p, but it takes you about two hours to produce, pack and deliver each item. You don't care because you are keen and eager. Orders take off. Soon, you are working flat out 60 hours a week, but you are stuck. You could employ someone else to do the work, but their hourly rate will be at least £6 (factoring in the national minimum wage and national insurance costs). Even by getting production time down to one hour, you are making a loss of £1.60 each hour this person works with you.

This all sounds obvious I know, but many people fall into this trap. Be careful to include:

- How much time realistically goes into each item. Include time to purchase your supplies, set-up time, packing and delivery time, how long it takes to invoice for each item, and then chase payment.
- Put in an honest rate for how much you would have to pay *someone else* to do your job. If yours is a specialist skill, or requires a unique blend of persuasive personality, don't assume you can get someone for £6 an hour to replace you.

♟ Entrepreneur's Secret for service businesses: How many *can* you sell?

If you are running a service business, you will be selling your own time. As an energetic entrepreneur, you will probably put the number of hours in the day as your work time. This is a mistake. You need to include travel time between jobs, seasonal fluctuations, holidays, customers missing appointments, time off to do your sales and book-keeping. A more realistic capacity is probably around 65 per cent. This also applies if you take on other members of staff.

2. Overhead costs

On top of the cost for producing each item, you will also have fixed or overhead costs that you will incur no matter how hard you work. Examples include rent for your premises, marketing costs, telephone, professional fees, car loans etc.

As the name implies, these costs will hang over your head regardless of how many fighting fish you sell. There will often be a few days of the week or months of the year where business will be slow. But your overhead costs won't go away. Therefore, it stands to reason you want to:

Keep your overheads as low as possible

Turn to Chapter 9 on 'Bootstrapping' for some advice on how to do this.

One of your most important overhead costs is you. Don't do what I did when I started out and forget to include your own salary and just take it from profits. The risk here is that there will often be no profits, and when there are, the temptation is to take them all out and buy yourself a shiny new TV.

First, work out your minimum survival budget. I wouldn't base it on an optimistic future assumption of how little you can get by on. Instead, look back at the last three months to see how much you've actually spent.

Then set this as a salary that comes out by standing order from your bank account. Get into the discipline of only increasing this when you know you can sustain it for at least four months. If you want a greater incentive, then pay yourself a sales bonus for each new piece of work you bring in.

Break-even point

Once you know how many you *could* sell, you need to work out how many you *must* sell to meet your overhead costs.

As well as a break-even price, there is also a break-even level of sales. As some of your costs are fixed overheads (in particular, the amount you need to live on), there is a minimum number of items you must sell in a year to cover your fixed costs. When you calculate your projections, make sure this level at least covers your overheads.

Business plan checklist

Now that you've thought about why and for whom you are putting this plan together, you are ready to draft your own. Overleaf is a simple checklist, or you can get similar forms from banks or enterprise agencies. But remember, this has to be your plan, not theirs.

Toolkit: On the *From Acorns* website (www.fromacorns.com) is a link to some bank business plan templates (if that's who you are approaching to raise finance).

What should go in your plan

Brief summary of your idea:
- What the market is, and why your idea is unique.
- Forecasted profits.
- Longer-term prospects.
- How much finance is required.

You and your team:
- Track record with key achievements for yourself.
- Other people who will be helping you.
- An honest appreciation of your strengths and weaknesses, and what you will do to bridge these.

Your product or service:
- A brief description of what it is and what needs it is servicing.
- Your target market (current size and your predictions on growth). Put the main points here and keep any detailed supporting statistics in the appendix.
- A more detailed analysis of the specific niche your product/ service will fit.
- Your competitors: who are the prime ones and how will you compete against them?
- What are the unique selling points of your product/service?
- A SWOT analysis: your strengths, weaknesses, opportunities and threats.

Sales and marketing:
- Your price, and how you decided on this.
- Place: where will you be selling your product from.
- Who will do the selling.
- What promotional plans you have.

Operations:
- Suppliers.
- Equipment needed.

Financials:

- Your forecasts, and the *evidence* behind your assumptions.
- Monthly cashflow forecast for year one, and quarterly for year two.
- Profit and loss forecast.
- Balance sheet.

CHAPTER 9

Lower-risk ways to start in business

Lower-risk ways to start in business

You have your idea and are ready to take the plunge. Now is the time to take a piece of wisdom from the mountaineer Chris Bonnington, (or more precisely – his mum):

💡   **Do dangerous things safely**

It's a great principle. Any muppet can pack in their job, remortgage their house and leap into a business without thought. It takes a much more canny operator to work hard to minimise all the risks before they start. This should become your mantra in every business endeavour.

There are some ways to do this when you start up.

Lower-risk start-up strategies

Get your existing employer to support you: A brilliant way to start is to have your current employer as your main customer. This is not as ludicrous as it may sound, and many entrepreneurs have started up this way. You might be taking away an unprofitable part of their business that they are happy to see the back of, or you might become a great supplier for them.

Corporate venturing/intrapreneurship: An alternative is to start up your business within the auspices of a large company. On one hand, you might have to accept a lower level of ownership of the business, and have to take on board a wider range of viewpoints when making your decision. On the other hand, they will support you through the critical start-up phase, give you access to a wide range of resources and hopefully provide your initial customers or leads. And at the end of the day, you might prefer 25 per cent of a £1 million company rather than 100 per cent of one which struggles to turn over £100,000.

But that said, don't forget there is one definite downside of starting a business as an employee:

"This may sound cheeky, but any tips on how to ensure I remain in control of my idea and ensure I receive a fair split of revenue generated when my employers might be underwriting the costs and risks?" (James, PR)

You said it. The person who takes the risk is the one who gets the greatest reward.

Keeping the day job?

"Should I keep the day job until I raise enough money?" (Muriel, designer)

Sounds reasonable? I'm not so sure. For a start, how much are you realistically going to save every month, and what difference will that make? What worries me more is the possibility that you'll never properly commit to your idea. See the quotation on page 206 for the importance of this. You'll get involved in your day job, and your idea will gradually whither on the vine. Preparation can only take you so far. There comes a point when you've got to swallow a brave pill and take the plunge.

Franchising

Franchising is simply using somebody else's system for running a business. This used to be looked down on, but there is absolutely no reason to be sniffy – there are over 30,000 franchised outlets in the UK and over 93 per cent claim to be profitable.

The benefits are that you are getting a tried and tested concept, and a proven brand, so you can hit the ground running and should have a more rapid build of turnover. You also get support, training and the chance to share best practice around a network.

Of course, this comes at a price. You will usually have to pay something like an initial franchise fee, a management services fee or royalty, an advertising levy and/or a product mark-up.

And this cost is not just financial. Running a franchise is more restrictive – the franchisor will have systems you will be expected to adhere to, performance levels you will have to meet, and they will be able to inspect you.

Generally speaking, if your primary concern in running a business is to earn a good regular income, then this is something you should look at seriously. If, on the other hand, you want a high degree of personal freedom and control, then perhaps it is not for you.

 Visit the British Franchise Association website (**www.british-franchise.org**) for an excellent range of information into all things franchising.

Of course, one of the lowest risk ways is not to take a financial risk. That brings us to bootstrapping.

The beauty of bootstrapping

The more upfront money a business requires, the less chance it has of getting off the ground. (Mark McCormack, What They Don't Teach You at Harvard Business School*)*

Bootstrapping is an American term for starting out with no money. Many large companies like Microsoft originally started up with just pennies. There is a lot to be said for bootstrapping the start of your business:

- You can make mistakes on the cheap. You will never get it right first time and without large debts you can change tack midstream.
- You don't know what your customers want until you actually start selling it to them. For example, you might have decided to open a retail outlet, only to find your customers are happier buying from you over the phone.
- You can give yourself time to deal with the Law of Unintended Consequences (see page 185). In other words, you have financial space to find out what customers really want from you.

- Surviving with little money gives you a good financial discipline as you grow.

Some bootstrapping techniques

Get your customers to pay for your set up: This might sound a little strange, but don't overlook your customers as a source of start-up finance. If you are developing a product that will lead to real cost savings or benefits for a client, and that doesn't exist somewhere else, see if the client will help fund the development by paying a deposit for the order.

> *A designer produced a prototype version of a Christmas card tree (for holding all your cards). She took it to a major retailer who loved it, and ordered 10,000. She then offered them a 10 per cent discount if they would pay a deposit upfront for the order, which they were happy to do. She used this to pay for her printing.*

Ask yourself, do you really need it? The best approach is to spend as little as possible. Think through every purchase you want to make and ask if it is essential. Do you have to have a brand new shiny computer/car, or can this wait? Do you need an office, or can you start off working from home (see the next section). Can you 'incubate' your business in the offices of a larger company? You will find many of your proposed outgoings are things you want rather than need for your start-up.

> *"I'd welcome your suggestions on how to raise finance. I want to build a flight simulator to get people over their fear of flying." (Angela)*

You've got to admire Angela's style and passion, but surely there must be a cheaper way to start up? You could mock-up a plane, perhaps get access to an unused plane? Use your creative powers not in raising money, but in reducing your start-up costs.

Don't buy outright: If you really need a major capital expenditure, see if you can rent, lease or borrow it rather than buy it outright. The temptation when you start out is to think you need to own all your equipment in order to function, but this just isn't true. By leasing your major purchases, you can update to better equipment quickly and cheaply when the money rolls in, or change quickly if your market is not where you thought it was.

Negotiate and shop around: Everything is negotiable. Always ask for a discount when you buy things. Ask if there is a discount for paying in cash, or paying early. The worst thing they can say is no.

Get good prices from your suppliers: People get so carried away in squeezing a few extra pennies from customers, they forget that saving money from your suppliers can have a huge impact on profitability.

Get them to do some creative thinking. Tell them what your budget is, and what your end product will do. Then ask them if they can think of any creative ways to deliver this.

Don't get lazy and stick with the status quo. Make sure that you shop around at least once a year to see if you can get better prices. At the very least, it will keep your current suppliers on their toes. Remember how much harder you'd work if your customers were regularly shopping around.

When negotiating with suppliers, you could borrow the 'daft lassie' technique:

> *A young woman built up a very successful jewellery business, starting from a market stall in Glasgow's Barrowland market. When negotiating with suppliers, and particularly professionals, she said she perfected the art of asking 'daft lassie' questions such as 'Instead of paying you an upfront fee, why don't you take a commission on what you save me?' The suppliers were amazed that no one had asked them before, and, as often as not, said yes.*

Working from home v. from an office

When starting out, consider working from home. It's not ideal, but if you have a couple of lean months you will not have to worry about rent and other associated costs.

David Jones set up his computer company, DMA Design, from his bedroom while still a computer science student. His first two games provided enough royalties to keep him going while he developed his third. This was Lemmings, and it sold 60,000 copies within a few days and went on to become a worldwide bestseller.

What is important is that you keep a separation between your home and work life. If possible, have one room that is exclusively used for work. Another tip from an entrepreneur is to consider 'commuting' to your home. Before you start work, at lunch time, and at the end of the day – get out of your house and go for a walk. This can be a great way to separate your two lives.

If you are taking on an office or premises, don't automatically go for an expensive city-centre location. Unless you are a retail business, in most instances you will have to visit your clients and not the other way round.

> 🏆 **Entrepreneur's Secret: Be very wary of signing long leases**
> You will not be able to escape these even if your business stops.

Of course, working from home can be a little difficult if you are taking on staff:

I remember interviewing for an early member of staff when I worked from home. I had done everything I could to disguise the fact that my bed was in the corner of the room. The whole way through the interview I had to repeat a mantra to myself, 'Don't glance at the bed, don't glance at the bed ...'

Avoiding partnershaft

I was delighted to learn that the German for partnership is *Partnerschaft*.

Many people are tempted to start up in partnership with someone to help reduce the risks. In an ideal world, this is because they have complementary skills. However, more commonly it is because they are afraid of doing it on their own.

But I'd like to sound a note of caution. I have seen many successful businesses torn apart by warring partners. The problem is that small business can place great pressures on people, and over time partners can grow apart. It's like marrying the first person you go out with. Try the following litmus test:

- Be honest with yourself, are you just doing this because you are nervous? Don't apologise for this, if you are not pretty wound-up going into business, you certainly ought to be. It's just that there are much easier ways of building up a support network that will give you everything a partner would.

- If you are doing it for strategic reasons, for instance you have different skills you could not find elsewhere, then draw up a detailed partnership agreement at the outset. This should cover exactly what the two (or more) of you are going to be specifically responsible for, and what you'll do if you change your minds in future. I know this feels a bit like drawing up a pre-nuptial agreement, but you can then file it in a bottom drawer and (hopefully) never look at it again.

There is an exception to this:

Going into partnership with your wife, husband or lover: This so goes against all rational business logic that it can often work extremely well in practice. I have seen many husband-and-wife partnerships that result in very fulfilling personal and business lives. Maybe it's because you've made such a commitment you have no option but to succeed?

However, it can add a certain extra stress to starting up:

> *"The hardest thing for me is getting the balance right between work and home and making the distinction between the two when you are working with your partner. The emotional conflict could be make or break for some people, and I would love to see a book truly acknowledging the emotional risk involved." (Mark)*

If you recognise this risk, then there are some things you can do to make this easier:

- Be as professional as possible: treat each other as employees.

Have clear job descriptions about where your roles and responsibilities begin and end. This extends to how you communicate with each other – you wouldn't call a member of staff 'a lazy good-for-nothing waste of space' (hopefully), so resist the temptation to do this to your partner.

- Keep work at work. I know a couple who have a line on their kitchen floor beyond which they are not allowed to discuss business. It's not such a bad idea, as otherwise your work worries will follow you everywhere.
- If you have staff, include them in communication. Bear in mind that for them it can feel as if there is a secret society which operates around the kitchen sink where all the real decisions are made. Try to keep to formal lines of reporting, and have regular meetings.

CHAPTER 10

Raising finance

Raising finance

Sometimes bootstrapping your birth would just compromise the development of your idea, so you have to spend money to make money. The following are the most obvious sources of finance.

Sources of finance

Your own savings: There is nothing like spending your own hard-earned dosh to really focus your mind. It is also a great sign to other investors, who are much more likely to come in if they can see you are taking an equal personal risk.

At the same time, keep some savings. It is a timeless rule of business that you will need more money than you anticipated. It also makes it much easier to sleep at night knowing you have a little emergency cash stashed away.

> **Entrepreneur's Secret: Make regular savings**
> Regularly put some savings into a 30-day notice account. They pay a little more interest but, more importantly, the notice period stops you from taking money out when you don't need to.

Tax rebate: If you have been paying tax for a few years, you might be able to claim a rebate on this if you don't make a profit in your first year.

Family and friends: You may think this is the cheapest source of money, and in real terms it often can be. However, the emotional cost of this can be huge. If you are going to borrow from friends and family, do it professionally. Draw up a simple agreement that says what they are getting for this investment and what the intended repayment schedule will be.

⚖ Entrepreneur's Secret: Beware credit cards

There are many stories of ballsy American entrepreneurs who start up by borrowing lots of money on credit cards. OK, it might be easy, but it is both incredibly risky and incredibly expensive. The risk is that you get stuck in a spiral of debt, using one card to pay off another and all the time facing interest rates of up to 20 per cent. You don't need that kind of stress!

Venture capitalists: Anyone who thinks throwing money at sexy start-ups is a good idea should read the excellent book *Boo Hoo* about the rise and fall of boo.com. There is a wonderful moment where the start-up almost doubled its valuation overnight when a venture capitalist misread the dollar sign in a fax for a pound sign, and then translated their valuation back into dollars. Exciting though the thought may be, it is highly unlikely you will get a venture capitalist to invest in your start-up venture. They have increasingly high investment thresholds and are typically looking for a three-exit for their investment (after three years they'll be looking to take their money back out of a business, so they'll either want to sell the business, sell their stake in it or float the business).

Far more interesting are:

Business angels: This is where the 'Dragon's Den' comes in. A business angel is normally a wealthy individual (or sometimes a consortium of individuals) who is investing for the longer term in your business. Like a venture capitalist, an angel will expect equity in the business. Their interest is usually more personal in the business, and they will get a range of tax breaks for their investment.

As important as the money is their expertise. A good business angel should come with a track record of building and possibly selling a business, and

In business, angels do exist

they can therefore hopefully guide you on your way. As well as a wise head, they will also come with a 'little black book' of contacts that can be invaluable to your business.

There are formal angel networks you can approach. Alternatively, you might know a wealthy individual who has perhaps made a capital gain recently and might be interested.

> *Iain McGlinn ran a small garage. He was approached by a friend who wanted to set up a beauty shop, so he invested £4,000 for 25 per cent. When the company, The Body Shop, was recently sold, Iain netted £150 million for his stake.*

The bank: Sooner or later, you will end up at the bank, either to deposit your well-gotten gains, or cap in hand to borrow money.

Many people are nervous about going to banks. The secret is to think of them as a 'money shop': they want to 'sell' money to good prospects – they only make a profit from the money they lend out and make interest on.

How to get a bank to lend you money

> *They give me an umbrella when it's dry and demand it back when it rains*

This is a consistent gripe against banks. During the last recession, there was an element of truth to this as many banks had made some bad lending decisions. However, since then they've tightened up their act. Anyway, they are businesses not charities. It's up to you to make sure this doesn't happen to you.

Do your homework: The first stage is to reassure them you are a good bet (look at Chapter 8 on the business plan). Present them with a professional image. Show them you have done your homework and take this seriously. It will also reassure them if you have a range of finance from different sources: your savings, other sponsors and orders from customers.

Shop around: As with anything else you are 'buying', it pays to shop around. If you don't get an offer, or you don't like the one you've got

– don't worry. There are plenty more sources of cash, and it will only cost you a bit of boot leather.

Ask early: If a friend came to you in desperation begging for urgent cash for their business, while sympathetic, wouldn't you be a little nervous about lending it to them? The trick is always to ask for more money than you might need, and ask for it early on. The bank will be far more impressed with your cautious approach, and your long-term planning.

Keep in touch: As with any customer or supplier, it is vital to keep a good relationship. When you win new work, tell your bank, or send them press cuttings. They are more likely to lend to someone they know, like and trust.

My room-mate from university, Matt, had a very good relation-ship with his bank manager. Every holiday, the manager would happily extend his considerable overdraft as Matt passed on stories and photographs of the exotic countries he'd visited in his breaks. Except the last time he returned, the manager had van-ished. Apparently he'd taken early retirement to go off travelling.

The Prince's Trust

If you are under 30 (or 26 in Scotland), the Prince's Trust and the Prince's Scottish Youth Business Trust are a fantastic source of support and finance when starting out in business. I got my start-up money from them, and have been a big fan ever since.

Their position is 'the lender of last resort' – they are there to lend money when you have exhausted all other sources. They also give you far more than the money, and it is almost worth borrowing money from them just to get access to all their services. You might also find other banks are willing to lend to you once the Trust is on board, as they respect their lending decisions.

"PSYBT gave me the support and finance I needed to start my business, when others would not help. Now, as a Board Member, I have a fantastic opportunity to help young people." (Michelle Mone, founder of the Ultimo bra)

Government support

The government's role is to step in where there is a gap in market provision.

Small Firms Loan Guarantee Scheme: This is one of the most popular support schemes. The government recognises some businesses will not be able to provide security for their borrowing, so under this scheme, if you can show that you have been refused funding because of a lack of security, the DTI (Department for Trade and Industry) can step in and guarantee 75 per cent of the loan, in return for a 2 per cent premium you pay them on the loan. You can apply for this scheme through your bank, who will guide you through the required stages.

Grants and 'free money':

> *"If I don't get a grant, I can't start in business." (Wendy, T-shirt business)*

Grants are the holy grail of start-ups, and sadly it is a myth to think there is a large amount of free money swilling around just waiting for the first clever person to ask for it. Often, if you spent as much time on reducing your start-up costs as you do in applying for grants, you wouldn't need one in the first place.

If you are determined to go this route, then a few words of advice:
- There is an art to applying. One theory as to why much of the Lottery grants goes to the South East of England is that the people there are very good at knowing how to fill out the application forms. It's the same with business grants. The process for doing this can be *very* laborious. With all the information you are going to have to provide, it's probably worth applying for a number of grants if it's going to be worth your effort.
- Ask around your local council. Grants come and go quite quickly. It's worth having a sniff around the 'Enterprise Department' of your local council to see if there's anything relevant to your specific circumstances.
- Look for 'support-in-kind'. There is a much wider range of non-direct assistance packages that can be just as valuable as cash.

This can include reduced cost staff who are getting into work, or returning to the workplace after having children. There are training courses, e-commerce schemes, assistance in exploring new export markets or registering patents and trademarks. Tap into this network as soon as you start your business plans by going through your Business Link in England, Business Eye in Wales, Local Enterprise Company in Scotland or Invest Northern Ireland in Northern Ireland (see page 207, Useful Contacts, for details).

CHAPTER 11

The dreaded legals

The dreaded legals

Most business start-up guides have acres of information on legal issues. Being all 'legalled-up' to the eyeballs will not make you a success. That said, ignoring the most basic legal issues can quickly put you under.

Red-tape busting

There is sadly a bewildering array of regulations facing the small business owner. This seems to be coupled with our adoption of the wonderful American 'blame, claim and gain' culture where you watch TV footage from Oklahoma of bystanders climbing onto a bus *after* it has crashed and then sitting down, start to rub their necks and complaining about whiplash.

We also seem to spend an inordinate amount of time worrying about things these days. It's not helped by HM Department of Vague Paranoia telling us to stock up on tinned peaches in case of an attack of rabid extremist chickens.

I say, stuff it. It's not worth worrying about the risks. There's not much you can do about it, and anyway there tend to be exemptions for smaller businesses. The greatest risk you can take is *not* doing something.

Take employment tribunals – the ultimate fear of any small business owner who watched too much *Crown Court* as a child. Statistics from the Employment Tribunals Service show that of the 115,042 claims brought in 2005, only 14 per cent were successful. Yet around 44 per cent of small companies settle

Don't worry - you can't protect yourself from *every* risk

out of court, not to mention the thousands who settled ages before in sheer unspecified terror.

Sometimes, it's better to beg for forgiveness than ask for permission.

There is an excellent government guide that gives an overview of the tax and legal issues for start-ups. You can get it from **www.hmrc.gov.uk/startingup/index.htm** or by calling 0845 915 4515.

Get a legal MOT

It is likely that at some stage you will require the use of a lawyer. The rule of thumb here is:

> **Use lawyers like condoms**

Lawyers are there to prevent problems from happening. I would advise you to see one now so that you don't have to see one later. Spending a bit of time at the outset can save you a huge amount of grief later. Also, like your prophylactics, don't just go for the cheapest – it can be tricky to get a refund if things go wrong later ...

> *For refund, insert baby. (Sign on condom vending machine in London underground)*

Ask your lawyer to do a legal MOT for you. My lawyers did this for me, and it was excellent value. It should take a maximum of two hours where they run through all the main risks and legal issues that you should be aware of, from the right legal form for your business to contracts, insurance, copyright and so on. At the end of this, you should have a checklist.

Don't panic! You don't have to deal with all of these immediately. Business is all about taking calculated risks, you just have to prioritise which ones you can deal with, and afford.

If a lawyer is not prepared to do this, then you should question whether they just want to get the maximum fees out of you.

Avoiding disputes

Most legal disputes seem to arise from two common causes, which you should avoid:

1. Poor communication: For example, agreeing a contract with a customer is just a process of talking through all the possible eventualities so there can be no misunderstanding in the future.
2. Ego: Many people take court action, because they feel aggrieved and bruised. Sure, you feel wronged, and it is like a slap in the face. But is it really worth it *for the business* to spend thousands of pounds and months of time taking someone to court? The risk is that you win the battle but lose the war.

> *A small software company found Microsoft had inadvertently copied one of their designs. Feeling aggrieved, they took the giant to court, and after a protracted battle, won their case. The company went bust shortly afterwards because of all the time the case took.*

 When seeking revenge, dig two graves

Should I be a limited company?

When you start in business, you can take two basic legal forms:

Sole trader (or partnership): This is the simplest form. It requires little or no paperwork, and is simplest from a tax point of view. A downside is that the business is you – there is no other distinct legal entity to protect you. Should you go bust, people can come after you personally for any debts you have.

It often makes sense to start as a sole trader or partnership (two or more people), but there's no reason why you shouldn't stay as one if you wish. John Lewis, the department store chain, is still a partnership.

Limited company: A limited company is a distinct legal entity separate from you, the individual (even if you own all the shares). You become an employee of the business, and are not automatically chased for all the debts if things go wrong. If, like me when I first realised this, you are thinking 'Why would anyone in their right minds *not* want to limit their liability?', then bear the following in mind.

- Given that you have a degree of protection, there comes an equivalent responsibility. You have to file your accounts at Companies House (which means your competitors can look at them), and beyond a certain turnover level, they have to be audited. Also, as a director, there are certain standards you have to comply with (such as not continuing to trade when you know you are insolvent). Failure to comply can result in legal action.
- There is also a very different tax regime as a company. Now you are taxed both on your salary (as any paid employee is) and, in addition, on the profits your business makes.
- As a limited company, you can issue shares to other people in your business.
- Finally, funders are obviously wise to the benefits of incorporation. They will therefore often expect you to give personal guarantees on any of your borrowings. So if your business loan is secured against your house – what limits on your liability do you *really* have?

There is no simple answer. You must speak to an accountant who can guide you through what is right for your personal circumstances and stage of business.

CHAPTER 12

Guerrilla marketing

Guerrilla marketing

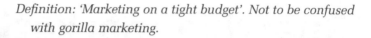

Definition: 'Marketing on a tight budget'. Not to be confused with gorilla marketing.

A hungry entrepreneur will be tempted to skip this section and go straight out selling. Before you do, consider:

 The smarter you are with your marketing, the easier your sales will be

A quick definition: Marketing covers everything required to get your product or service to meet a customer's need. It is taught as the 4 Ps:

- your **P**roduct (or service)
- the **P**lace you sell it from
- your **P**rice
- finally, **P**romotion, or how you get your customers.

Let's look at each in turn, starting in this chapter with your product.

Your product or service

You may think you know what product or service you are going to offer, but just consider the following few points:

 A customer is not interested in your product/service – they are interested in what it can do for them

Forget features – sell the benefits: If this sounds obvious, then think, why are computers always sold just on the size of their hard drive and whizzy technical specifications? Look at Apple Computers who, when they launched their iMac computers, had the genius to make them visually stunning, and bring them out in a range of 'flavours' (and the lime-flavoured version sold out). When you get too close to your product, it is easy to forget what the actual benefits are to your customers.

 Toolkit: The following exercise, the: 'Acme Benefit Generator' should help you.

Make a list of five features of your product or your service in the first column. In the second column, add in the benefit of each feature to your client. These benefits are how you should describe and market your business.

Feature	Benefit
Example: I use a stronger wood to make my furniture	*Which means for the customer:* Furniture built to last you a lifetime
1.	
2.	
3.	
4.	
5.	

Once you have a list of benefits, these and not the features should form the basis of your marketing.

Understand what business you are in: I know this sounds stupid, but consider:

> *Parker Pens revolutionised their business when they realised they were not a pen company but a gift company. Customers tended to buy their pens as presents, and in that case their nearest competition was not other pens but golf clubs, wallets and carriage clocks.*

This is an extension of the last exercise, but you have to ask yourself continually what people are *really* buying from you.

> *Jennifer thinks people will come to her café because it's cheap. But perhaps they just want a break from the office at lunchtime. In that case, why not put out a plentiful supply of newspapers and comfy chairs? Part of the success of Starbucks is not the coffee, rather, it is being the 'third place', i.e. not home and not the office, where people can have a rest. Or perhaps office workers are very pushed for time? In which case, why not offer to deliver the food to their office? And while you're at it, why not offer them pre-cooked fresh food they can heat up for their supper?*

What do people really want from your gardening service: just someone else to do the back-breaking labour, or is it botanical knowledge, or creative flair? Depending on which it is, you could offer a service for other labour-intensive jobs, or a free design consultation, or a regular mailer on which plants are in season.

Don't just be blinkered by what customers have bought in the past, or what your competition is doing – think what they *might* want but no one has thought to offer them.

Be different: You can gain a great advantage over your competitors not by spending huge amounts on marketing, but just by being different from everyone else. The more unique the selling point of your product, the easier it is going to be for you to sell. Of course, this has to be an advantage that offers real value to your customers. If your only advantage is a cheaper price, it is going to be a long hard slog for you.

You can be different in any number of ways. It could be the way your product is delivered:

> Peter Wood became a multimillionaire and revolutionised the centuries-old insurance industry. How? He just used a bright red telephone. But before Direct Line, no one else had thought of selling insurance direct to customers over the phone.

It could be an extra added feature of your product that no one else offers:

> A carpet-fitting company offered computer-aided design for hotels. Previously, to fit new carpets, a hotel would have to shut for days just to do the measuring. With the new service, this could all be planned in advance by computer, resulting in only half the closure time. This had huge benefits for customers.

It can simply be the way your product is packaged:

> When Belinda Jarron set up her business supplying plants and flowers for offices, she decided to call it Fleurtations. She painted her vans bright pink and gave her staff colourful outfits. One of her main competitors is Rentokil, so it is easy to see how this might be an advantage.

One of my favourite entrepreneurs is a Scots-Italian called Gio Benedetti. He has made 'difference' his mantra, and made a lot of money along the way.

> His latest business is a redesign of the humble first-aid box. The traditional green box hasn't been redesigned for decades. Gio has launched a new one. It is based on the shape of his Porsche and the smooth opening device is modelled on the ashtray of his Jaguar (see what I mean about the entrepreneur bit). There is a thermometer strip on the outside, and lots of easy tape dispensers. Sure, it costs a bit more than the old one, but it is so much easier to use, and is now sold in stores around the UK.

Building a big brand on a small budget

You've got your product/service – now you have to give it a brand. Most of you will now think – 'Hmm, branding sounds like a big expensive word for a small business, maybe I'll skip this section'. Stick with me on this one.

Take a couple of moments now to think back to the last major purchase you made. I bet at the time there was a real feeling of excitement? I would also wager that by about now, there is also a considerable degree of fear; have I bought the right one, will it break down, could I have bought it cheaper?

Buying stuff is scary. Over many years of selling, and listening to others, I have come to the following, rather cynical conclusion:

> **People often don't want the best – they want the least worst**

The number of times I've heard of someone who lost work when the client said, 'You were the best proposal, but we went with someone who was bigger'. It makes me want to scream and start to gnaw my leather restraining straps.

This is what a brand is – it is about trust. In a confusing and increasingly busy world, customers want to plump for what they feel safest with. Your challenge in a small business is to reassure them that they're making a smart decision.

Smoke and mirrors – the Wizard of Oz approach to branding

An American entrepreneur was starting a document storage business. The problem was that he had very few clients. When prospects visited his warehouse, they saw row after row of empty shelves. It didn't exactly inspire confidence. So, taking the 'Wizard of Oz' approach literally, he lined the walls of the warehouse with mirrors behind the boxes he had, and used a few blank ones. Hey presto – prospects walked in, saw the place was packed, and gave him the order.

Now, I'm not saying you should ever lie about things (heaven forbid!). I'm just saying that sometimes you can allow your prospects to come to the conclusion that you are larger than you actually are.

We were in the running for a large marketing contract from a bank. They said they wanted to come meet us at our office. We guessed they were worried we might be too small to handle it, so we quickly 'hired' some friends to boost our staff. The client seemed happy, and we were given the contract, which naturally we did a great job on. Fortunately they didn't notice people putting corrector fluid on their screens, reading things upside down, or the fact we'd somehow employed twin sisters.

Remember, while a customer wants the best product, they don't want to feel stupid when they get your product back home, or when they tell everyone else in the office. There's a mantra that 'No one ever got sacked for buying IBM'. This hasn't arisen by accident. IBM has spent millions researching things like the exact colour of their logo, 'IBM Big Blue', which gives the most calming thoughts to the viewer.

Of course, if you are a scary, innovative and different company, then you have to make customers feel the biggest risk is *not* buying from you and going with something boring. This requires hype – which we cover later.

Branding rules

Consistency: A famous French chef was asked the secret of his success. He answered:

Excellence is the sum of many small things superbly done.

To reassure your clients, look after the little pieces. This doesn't have to mean big expense. Make sure your phones are answered consistently, your logo is applied consistently on letters, envelopes, signs, uniforms and invoices. Sandwich chain Pret A Manger go as far as sprinkling their logo in chocolate on the foam on your cappuccino.

Nextdoor.com design and manufacture doors. Despite them being a small business, you are immediately impressed by their professionalism. In their shop, all the staff wear the same outfits, the fitters have overalls with corporate branding, as do the vans, which are always bright and clean. This gives great reassurance to customers that they are dealing with a professional outfit.

Your business has one huge branding advantage – you: Don't always hide behind a big 'corporate' identity. Customers like the fact that it's your raggedy butt on the line if things go wrong. They know where you live and can phone you up at 3.00 a.m. and demand delivery. Bring more of yourself and your own personality into the brand.

Alistair Rutherford built up Edinburgh Preserves selling home-made chutneys. After a few years of hard graft they started getting orders from the big supermarkets. Al decided it was time to become a bit more professional. He brought in a design agency to produce new labels and packaging. When he showed these to the supermarket buyer, they were horrified and made him dump them. The reason his products sold so well was precisely because they didn't look mass-produced!

Be original: We are swamped with marketing. To cut through this noise, you need to be original.

A couple of years ago we launched an e-commerce magazine. There are over 1,000 business magazines in the UK, and it is reckoned you need a marketing budget of £700,000 to launch a new one. We had £700. I decided to launch it by spending a week living in a shop window surviving off the internet. I started in my pyjamas, with a credit card and computer in a shop window in Sauchiehall Street in Glasgow.

I had a number of challenges to complete. I had to order food (£40 from Iceland – a lot of food, no freezer). I organised a dinner party. I got a barber to come in, a 6-foot wooden giraffe, pipe band and vintage Bentley. The only challenge I failed was from my dear sister – to get a glass of ice.

I also drew quite a crowd. I had two drunks who adopted me and would post sandwiches through the letterbox every day. I got my own stalker who would smile enigmatically, and a group of night clubbers – one of whom shouted something about a 'job' she would give me if I let her in – I couldn't quite work it out.

Of course, this wasn't an exercise in e-commerce, it was an exercise in hype. I was in all the main papers (I got my three-month-old daughter in the Sun), on TV, had a radio station actually in the window with me, and about 1,000 emails a day. We also got more subscribers than any other Scottish magazine launch.

Think American: When you get first-hand experience of American businesses, you realise that often it is not that they are miles better than everyone else, it is just that they are miles better at creating the impression they are.

Sure, modesty is an endearing quality in a date, but it doesn't work for companies. Get testimonials from every other client you work for. Try to get some 'big names' on your client base even if, say, all you do for IBM is sweep their car park.

What name for your business?

Given all that we have talked about here, ideally your company name will be an embodiment of your brand.

Don't worry if you've picked a name and it's not the most imaginative – it won't stop you. Tesco was named after the founder's wife, Tessa Cohen. However, the right name can give you an advantage.

Reassurance: If you are sure this will be a major factor in the success of your business, then it makes sense to pick a reassuring name. An estate agency wanted a name that implied Scottishness, wisdom and wealth – they picked Stuart Wise Ogilvie. However, don't get too stuck on being safe – Branson has had no problem branding an airline Virgin.

If your brand is you: Since you are your business's greatest asset, there is merit in putting you as your company name. Many consultancies, whether advertising, legal or design, are named after their founders. Be aware that you will then become the embodiment of this brand, which is fantastic if you are outgoing, but a possible worry if you are more retiring by nature. And think what happens when you come to sell the business.

Memorable: If reassurance or individual service is not the most important thing for your business, then go for something memorable. If you can make people smile or think deeply, they will remember your name. This will make your marketing so much easier. Here are some good examples.

• An independent TV company called Extra Vegetables:

The founder had been on a BBC shoot, and the producer was apparently really stingy with the expenses. That night in the bar they had a few extra drinks, and listed them all on the receipt as 'extra vegetables'.

Caspian Woods

"Let me hold your balls for you"

Flat 6
75 Broughton Street
Edinburgh
EH1 3RJ

Tel: 031 557 8549
Fax: 031 557 9151

• An event organiser called 'Let me hold your balls for you':

This was actually one of my first businesses. I got the work, but also received a few extra unexpected offers as well.

• An IT consultancy called 3 Frogs:

Three frogs sit on a log, one decides to jump off, how many are left? Three – making a decision does not imply action. This consultancy's focus was in making IT projects actually happen.

Beware of boring acronyms: I'm not a fan of businesses named after a load of initials. And bear in mind the fate of the venerable Department of Trade and Industry (DTI) which changed its name to the Department for Productivity, Energy and Industry. It rapidly changed back five days later when a few naughty journalists started taking great joy in its possible new acronyms, DIPPY and PENIS.

Name it after the benefit you will give customers:

Don't call your business after who you are, but name it after
what you do, or you will confuse people. (Simon)

A good point from Simon. Try not to go for the obvious, like calling
your training company Aspire (apologies if that's you), but try something a little more memorable.

After all, Carphone Warehouse doesn't sell many carphones and
it's not in a warehouse, but that doesn't seem to have harmed them.

CHAPTER 13

Your place or mine?

Your place or mine?

It's a well-known saying that the three most important ingredients in a retail business are 'location, location and location'.

The problem is that the expense of getting the right location for your business can be prohibitive. A recent programme on the coffee phenomenon in the UK found that only one chain was actually consistently profitable. In the massive land-grab to get the best locations, most of the chains ended up paying so much in rent that their profits were all but wiped out.

Getting a good location without paying the earth

Become a destination store: If people are prepared to travel to you, then you don't have to be located in prime retail space. Clearly, this is not easy, and not for every business. It depends on how distinctive you make your business. People might travel a few miles for an award-winning restaurant, but not for a café.

> *Slaters Menswear has a policy of picking slightly out of the way retail spaces. They tend not to be on the main streets, or if they are, they'll be up on the second floors of buildings. What distinguishes them is the absolutely first-class customer service they give. This has helped them grow to become one of the largest menswear retailers in the UK.*

Is 'busy' enough? Many start-ups will choose their site by counting the number of people going past a particular unit at a given time of day. However, have you noticed in your town the 'white elephant' units that never seem to work for any business? Just because they are in a busy place, doesn't mean they'll work. There might be a huge footfall outside a busy train station. However, the chances are that most people are on their way home or dashing to work – they won't have time to sit down for a leisurely lunch.

Pay heed to the dictum:

> **If you want to open a restaurant, open it next door to a successful one**

Can the mountain come to Mohammed? Can you go direct to your customers rather than wait for them to come to you? If you have a sandwich business, why not deliver sandwiches direct to people's desks? Could you deliver your products by mail order, scooters, the phone or the web (see below)?

Co-partner: Consider opening up in other complementary places. Costa Coffee has opened units in bookshops, estate agents, banks and large offices.

> *One young entrepreneur opened a Japanese noodle bar in the spare area of a pub. Instead of rent and upkeep, they both share the profits. As a result, he has a massive captive clientele, less fixed costs and fewer of the worries of his own unit.*

Remote selling – e-commerce, phone and mail order

Are all dot.coms doomed? After the great dot.com euphoria, too many people shook their heads, saying 'never again'. History should teach us otherwise. The railway revolution at the end of the nineteenth century heralded a similar investment boom, and an equally precipitous bust. However, after this initial over-exuberance, nobody can deny that the railways ('just another route to market' – as nay-sayers dismiss the internet) had a radical impact on trade, and transformed certain industries.

As well as using websites as an online brochure (which we cover on pages 141–2), e-commerce has great potential for small businesses.

It might give you the chance to enter new markets (especially over-seas), it might allow you to build a stronger online brand than larger competitors, or it could help you undercut competitors by stream-lining your production process.

Similarly, I know a number of small businesses that started off trading on eBay before opening their own websites, and then their own physical stores. Others still sell excess stock on eBay as a side-line to their main businesses.

At the same time, e-commerce is not the only game in town. The telephone has revolutionised the insurance industry, and mail order is making continual inroads in retail.

Is it right for your business? As we saw on page 84, you have to be sure *exactly* what business you are in.

The internet was meant to be the death of retailers. This ignores the fact that for some types of goods, retail is therapy. This is why Waterstones was not killed off by Amazon. I use Amazon to search for specific titles that I can wait for, I go into Waterstones because it's a haven when I'm out shopping and I can wander aimlessly and walk out with completely random titles. Make sure you know exactly what needs you are satisfying for your customers.

Conversely, you might think that there are areas of your industry where retailers are not adding any value. This has happened to many brokers such as insurance, travel and stockbrokers. You might be able to build a great business by giving customers a cheaper way of missing them out.

What to avoid if you are selling online: Having spent a week living in a shop window off the internet, I feel in a good position to rant about what to avoid in sites. There is a large problem of 'trolley aban-donment' – people who get so fed up with a website purchase that they just give up. This is up to 50 per cent of purchasers in some big companies. This is people in the store, with their trolley full and wallet out, yet the rest of the experience frustrates them so much they walk out. The simple rule is KISS: **K**eep **I**t **S**imple **S**tupid. It includes:

- Avoid complex animation: Imagine you go to your local shoe shop. You are stopped at the front door, and asked if you can wait a couple of minutes while they get ready. Then when you walk into the store they run around with flags welcoming you into the store. Don't.

- Don't hide the till: Make your online ordering obvious and as simple as humanly possible. In particular:
- Avoid passwords: I don't need a secret password to walk into my local Tesco store, so why do so many sites require one? I understand where secure transactions are required, but it is too much to expect someone to do just for some editorial. I must have registered at hundreds of sites and there is a limit to how many memorable dates, places and names of pets that I can think of.
- Make sure the shop doesn't fall apart: I'm glad that sounds so obvious. I am still amazed at the number of airlines whose sites have glitches, or crash. I got an email from one of Britain's leading airlines last week. The reply address is blackhole@xxx.com. How reassuring is that?
- Don't build it and assume they will come: Just because you have a catchy name and a funky site, the world will not beat a path to your door. Even throwing millions at advertising won't make this happen. The same rules of marketing apply. Push your customers to your site, make sure it appears high up in search-engine rankings, get reciprocal links with other sites, and put your web address on all correspondence.

Don't be seduced by the promises of technology

CHAPTER 14

Getting your price right

Getting your price right

Getting your price right is hugely important. A 10 per cent increase in your price can increase your profits by as much as 40 per cent.

Setting the right price can be a tricky process. This is because price is tied up with the whole notion of 'worth' and is a very emotional issue. People often find it hard to ask a fair market price for their product or service because deep down they have a low sense of their own self-worth.

To get round this whole emotional minefield, people (and far too many business books) rely on technical pricing solutions. The most obvious version is 'cost-plus' pricing. Simply, you add up all your costs and then stick a margin on the top. While very tempting and easy, it is wrong for a basic reason:

 The right price is what your customer is willing to pay. Your costs only tell you if you have got a good deal from your suppliers

When publishing yearbooks, I realised I could make my books hardback, which would cost an extra £1 each, but as a result I could sell them for double the price – an extra £8. At the same time, my sales went up! People felt these were higher quality books and this was a small price to pay for keeping the memories of their friends and university safe for years to come. Which is also why I called the company Time of Your Life.

Six reasons not to be cheap as chips

Believe me, there is nothing sadder than sitting on a funding panel and hearing someone saying 'and we will win lots of customers by being the cheapest'. As well as implying something about the person's sense of self-esteem, it can cause a lot of business problems.

1. As a small business it's unlikely you will have the economies of scale (like purchasing power) to undercut everyone else indefinitely. You will probably only succeed in doing this by working yourself to the bone until you get complete burnout.

2. Don't forget, your competitors will react. If you start scooping up new customers, you run the risk of triggering a price war. They will probably have deeper pockets and more established customers than you, and in the end no one will win.

3. Once you have established a low price with a customer, it is very difficult to raise the price later. Imagine trying to increase your price by 30 per cent with an existing customer – they'll turn round and say 'What kind of mug do you take me for?' The same applies with 'Sales' in shops – do it too much and customers will just sit tight knowing another one will be along soon.

4. Bear in mind – customers have an irksome habit of talking to each other. If you drop the price for one, be very sure everyone else won't find out.

5. Low price and good value are not the same thing. Don't think that if you drop your price, customers will immediately beat a path to your door. Far more likely, they might think you are cheap and nasty and avoid you like the plague.

6. You risk ending up with just the cheap customers, who will dump you as soon as the price goes up.

   A number of hungry American credit-card companies came into the UK market keen to grab customers with zero-rate interest deals. The idea was that having hoovered up a big market share they could put their rates up. The problem was that they mainly got 'promiscuous' customers hungry for a good deal, who of course moved on to the next zero-rate deal when they put their rates up.

The perils of 'over-trading':

> *"Our diary is booked up three months in advance. We're working all hours. Customers are leaving us because they don't want to wait that long. We're skint, and have little to show for our efforts. My husband's thinking of jacking it in." (Michelle)*

I almost wanted to cry at that email. She is so passionate about her business. But, brushing aside the tears, I then wanted to shout very loudly – 'YOU ARE TOO CHEAP!' Such 'over-trading' sinks too many start-up businesses. It's a mixture of great enthusiasm and a lack of confidence.

If you put your prices up, you'll lose a few customers, but probably only the same number who were leaving you anyway as they were bored waiting. You'll have money to expand, and you'll feel better about yourself. Your 'lost' customers might well come back when they see the inferior service they get elsewhere.

Pricing strategies

I've interviewed hundreds of entrepreneurs, and the message that comes back loud and clear is: 'If you've got your product or service right, then price will be third or fourth on your list of customer's concerns'.

Your customers should squeak at your price: This is an acknowledgement that while your price is uncomfortable, it is only uncomfortable because your customers still want your product. You can then make them feel a little better about it by offering them a special discount such as free delivery or a free carrier bag. This allows customers to feel better about the whole thing and convince themselves mentally that actually they've got a great bargain. (If they actually scream and run from the building, then you've possibly gone a bit far.)

A great thing to point out to customers is:

> *You can have good quality, you can have fast, and you can have cheap. You can have any two of these you choose, but you cannot have all three. Which do you want?*

See how elastic your customers are: An unusually sexy term from economics, 'elasticity' is a measure of how far you can push certain customers before they snap. You'd be surprised how far certain customers will go. Who would have thought we'd be happy to pay £2.50 for some coffee beans and hot water, or £20 for withered flowers at an airport? You will often find your most elastic customers where there is a deeper need you are meeting that you might not have realised (i.e. feeding an addiction in the case of coffee, or marriage guidance counsellor in the flower scenario). Look at Chapter 12 for 'Understand what business you are in', page 84.

Set fire to your price list: Different people will pay different prices, in different places, in different seasons, at different times of the day, for a whole host of different reasons. People will pay double the price for a hardback book, mainly because they are desperate to read it before anyone else.

In an ideal world you would be able to price according to each and every customer's degree of need. This is, of course, fiendishly difficult to do and remember (though certainly doesn't mean you shouldn't try).

Start by trying different prices depending on the type of customer (i.e. a cheaper price to trade customers than to ordinary punters). Then try different pricing for different geographical markets, then perhaps for timing.

> As a small Scottish marketing agency, I once quoted a job for a
> friend in a big London-based agency. He phoned me up, chuck-
> ling 'Caspian, you idiot, you've sent me your costs – I need your
> prices'.

When you get more experienced in this, you can start to become a Jedi Price Master and read each customer coming through the door and price according to their level of desperation.

Don't win every customer: It is much better to have five customers paying you £20 an hour than ten paying £5.

Price your offering on what it saves your customers, not what it costs you

For example:

> *An oil services business specialised in stopping 'gushers' – whereby oil escapes uncontrollably from a well. They used to price their service on the cost of their travel and then an hourly rate for their service. A consultant pointed out that the cost per hour to the oil company of a gushing well was in the tens of thousands of pounds. The company therefore repriced their offering based on how much their prompt action saved their customers.*

This explains why emergency plumbers charge so much.

Trade your customers up:

> *You can normally buy a beefburger from a fast-food joint for 99p, but can you remember the last time you actually did? They make their money by trading people up to the Super Dooper meals and Extra Everything or Go Fat, which is where they make the money while still keeping the impression they are cheap.*

Think how many times you have been tempted into a shop by a low price in the window, only to be sweet-talked by a salesperson, and end up leaving the shop weighed down with expensive goodies. This should be your policy.

An alternative, and I think slightly dishonest approach, is to hook customers with extras. Think of all the extended warranties you get in electrical shops. Ever wondered why buying refill razor blades is more expensive than buying the original razor? My view is you may get customers once, but they'll get wise.

Never underestimate your customers' willingness to trade up

Tell your customers to BOGOF: A variation on the previous strategy, this wonderful acronym from the retail trade means Buy One Get One Free. This, and its multiple variations (25 per cent larger, third one free, etc.) is a good way to allow customers to feel they've got a good deal, while keeping up the value perception of your product.

Fixed or hourly price?

"Should I charge customers an hourly rate or a fixed fee?"
(Catrin, event organizers)

An advantage of an hourly rate is that if a job overruns (which they always do), then you'll recover your costs. It also gives you scope for negotiation.

Rather than say, 'This job will cost you £800', say, 'I'm worth £80 an hour and I estimate it will take me 10 hours to do'. Very few people will argue with your confident assertion of your worth, but they might try to haggle you down on the hours. That can be fine if you genuinely can do it faster. But otherwise, you can agree to fewer hours, but point out that if it does take longer, they'll be charged.

The downside is that customers are nervous about entering such an open-ended agreement (see below). It also ties how much profit you make as a company with how many hours you can work, and staff you can employ. If you charge a fixed fee, there's a chance to make a much larger net profit, but a bigger risk.

Therefore, perhaps go for a mixed approach. Make sure you've got your 'bread and butter' work on an hourly rate, so you know you can cover your bills. Then include the odd fixed-price job with the chance to make larger profits.

> ### ⚓ Entrepreneur's Secret: Manage your customers' expectations
>
> If you are charging on an hourly basis and it goes over what the client is expecting, be sure to let them know the moment it happens. The secret here is that even if it feels painful at the time, warning your clients early about potential overruns will save you huge grief in the long run. For example, if you tell a client their job is going to be a week late, and then it's only four days late – they'll be happy. But if you fail to tell them, even if it only ends up being two days late – they'll be very annoyed.

"How much should I charge my first customers?" (Rebecca, marketing consultancy)

New customers don't know anything about you, and are likely to be slightly nervous about entering into an open-ended agreement with you. The 'foot in the door' marketing technique would therefore say, give them a simple, fixed-price and low-cost introductory product or service. You can trade them up to a more flexible arrangement once you've established a relationship.

What if my industry is VERY price-sensitive?

Customers are savvy and are very willing to shop around, particularly using the internet. This can make certain businesses frighteningly price-sensitive. So what can you do?

- Specialise in a niche, not the mass market: It might be uncomfortable at first, but it can be far more pleasurable to have a small but highly profitable specialist niche in a market where you can keep your operations small, and lovingly craft your product.

  The pressure of cheaper Chinese-produced shoes has eroded the UK shoe manufacturing industry. However, a growing number of small British manufacturers make a very good living from handcrafted shoes sold around the world at up to £1,000 a pair.

Perhaps you can find a new market where the competition is a bit less intense

- Add non-core items: See if your customers will pay more if you add extra benefits to your service such as delivery, specialist packaging, installation services or after-sales support.
- Be entrepreneurial in finding supplies: Look hard at new technologies or new markets for getting suppliers. If you're getting hammered by Chinese competitors – join them. Source your supplies from there. It's easier than you think.
- Stress your added value: You might be able to justify a higher price if you can clearly demonstrate that you add more value than your competitors. Perhaps it's your after-sales service that customers' value, or your guarantees?
- Get out: Maybe you've inherited a business, or started up in a trade you have always been in. Unfortunately, just because there was a future for your business yesterday doesn't mean there will be one tomorrow. However much people lament the hordes of industrious Chinese who will work 50 times harder for a bowl of rice, they aren't going to go away. There are 1.3 billion of them.

CHAPTER 15

Getting your customers

Getting your customers

You've got your idea, funding, marketing, premises. You are ready to get cracking. Now comes the important stuff.

 Sales are the single critical success factor in your business

Customers are the fuel for your spaceship. It doesn't matter how wonderfully packaged your product, how good your systems, how well kept your books. If you don't have any fuel, you're going nowhere.

Put aside the myth that if you build a better mousetrap, your customers will beat a path to your door. I met a business which is a very salutary example of this.

> *There is a group of four incredible boffins running a fabrics company. They have taken fabrics to an extreme level. In amongst high-tech medical fabrics and bandages, they have developed part of a propulsion system for the space shuttle, and a new suspension system used on London taxis. They also invented a new design for an airbag and the company which bought it kitted out an assembly line with 100 staff to mass-produce it. Yet until recently they were living in an attic eking out a living. The reason – they were hopeless at selling their products.*

But before you rush out and leaflet the town, you need a logical and systematic approach. This is because of the importance of the number 4.

The magic number 4

I've got an old Renault, reasonable condition, looking for £1,200, do you want it?

What, who, hey, hold on a second ...

You cannot make someone buy something the first time they've heard of it. One nugget I got from four years of a business studies degree was being introduced to a lovely lady called AIDA. She works something like this:

- The first time someone hears about your business, they have **A**wareness.
- The second time they hear this might have heightened to **I**nterest (or, better yet, they are **I**ntrigued).
- The third time they hear, they might have actual **D**esire for your product or service.
- But only on the fourth contact will they finally take any **A**ction.

This translates into the fact that:

> **80 per cent of sales come after the *fourth* contact you make with a prospect**

"People are hearing about us through advertising and PR, but actually getting them to sign up is very hard." (Janet, children's cookery courses)

Many businesses make the mistake of putting a massive amount of money into one piece of marketing, like PR or press advertising, and then sit back to wait for the customers to roll in. Like Janet, they've done a great job at the early stages, but their customers are only at Interest or Desire. You need to do more marketing to push them into Action.

Someone might see your flyer sitting on their doormat, and register a vague awareness before stepping over it. Then they might read something about you in the local paper and actually have a desire to use your service, but still not pick up the phone. It is only when you give them a call that this turns to action, and they finally purchase your product.

So, whatever field your business is in, you need a sales funnel.

The sales funnel

Most classically trained sales professionals work with a sales funnel. As the name suggests, imagine a large funnel into which you start dripping not water but customers until the funnel starts to fill up, and they eventually come out the other end as sales.

Now, being canny entrepreneurs, why should we start at the wide end of the funnel – advertising, direct mail, websites which will take a few weeks/months/days to trickle down? No, let's start with the bit where we will get our quickest sales: people who already know and trust us.

Identifying your first leads

Unless you have very rich backers (or you are a dot.com), your sales approach should be that of a sniper and not a shotgun (apologies for the analogy). Don't say, 'Well, my customers could be everyone'. That's very nice for your ego, but it's not much use in focusing your sales.

You need to identify who your most likely customers would be. These are people you can get to trust you the quickest. These are people who already know you, or have worked with you, or who you know will trust you quickly. If you have no warm prospects like this, then you need to draw up a profile based on factors such as their location, their budget and their life stage.

You might also know customers from your competitor's business who might switch. OK, so that sounds a bit naughty, but this is business. For a start, you know these people have the budgets, and are interested in the product. There might be smaller customers your competitor is not as interested in. You never know, your competitor might even be interested in you taking them off their hands – stranger things have happened.

> **♟Entrepreneur's Secret: Watch out for change**
> A great number of products and services are bought during periods of change. This could be a life change like moving house, or having a baby (a huge time for camcorder sales). Alternatively, in company sales it could be when a new person takes over purchasing, a company is bought over, or identifies a new strategic direction.

Look for news stories, job announcements in the trade papers, even personal ads in the papers. Also look at other routes to these people. You could approach local estate agents and through them offer new house purchasers a free consultancy on garden design.

Conversely, if your contact in a company is moving – WATCH OUT. Don't assume the new contact will want to carry on working with you, they might have a pet supplier. Get in touch with them as soon as they arrive, and go back to stage one to build a relationship.

CHAPTER 16

How to become a hot sales person without selling your soul to Lucifer

How to become a hot sales person without selling your soul to Lucifer

The single most important skill you will need in your business is knowing how to sell.

Many famous entrepreneurs are glorified hustlers. Marks & Spencer started as market barrow boys. Richard Branson started in a telephone box. However, a lack of sales ability is probably the main cause of new businesses going under.

> *"We started ten months ago and I've been diligently filing 'nil' tax returns to the Inland Revenue ever since. The reason is that I'd prefer to plunge my right arm into a burning fire than make any cold calls!" (Bryan, engineering)*

Selling, like public speaking, is usually the one aspect of business that fills people with dread. But you don't have to be a 'born salesperson'; you can learn to be good at sales.

Being a good sales person does not require you to
a) lose your morals and integrity
b) have a personality bypass
c) wear red braces.

It does however involve one single hurdle. You must:

Prepare yourself for rejection

Sir Tom Farmer started his Kwik-Fit car servicing empire from a single business unit. One of his first sales approaches was to telephone large corporate buyers and sell to them. However, he found he got a high proportion of knock-backs. So he studied his approach – was it timing, was it his price, was it his competition? After trying lots of different approaches, he found that, no matter what, his ratio stayed at about 20 calls to every sale. So, he changed his attitude. 'I learned to stop worrying about all those noes and to get through them as fast as possible so I could get to the yeses.'

Brace yourself – people will reject you. The secret is not to take it personally

Don't worry if you'd rather eat your shoes than make a cold call to a stranger – so would most sane people.

The reason we don't like selling is that we don't like personal rejection. Psychologists reckon we take around 50 per cent of our sense of identity and self-worth from what others around us tell us – no person is an island. If you are selling, you're going to encounter a fair bit of rejection. If you keep getting knocked back, you are going to feel miserable after a while. Except for sociopaths, we all have a certain level of self-esteem – mojo if you like – and this goes up and down depending on feedback from others. See Chapter 25 for some medicine for your mojo.

But – in terms of selling – bear the following in mind:

> ## As any Casanova at your local nightclub will tell you: it's a numbers game

My best mate Paul snogged Carol Glaister. I'd fallen in love with her at about 13 years old, and worshipped her from afar throughout one hot summer. Then we went to the cinema with my mate Paul, and halfway through they started snogging. I was heartbroken. The thing was – Paul was in the habit of asking girls and not really being fazed if they said no. And he looked like a monkey.

You have to kiss a lot of frogs before you get your prince or princess. It's the same with selling. The secret is to take these rejections in your stride and *don't take them personally*.

The following are some ways to do this:

Keeping your pecker up

It's mostly a matter of timing:

> *We did some research into why our customers had bought from us. Was it our cutting-edge thinking, our keen pricing, the fact we were all-round great guys? Time after time, our clients said 'Well, you just happened to call us at the right time'.*

Most sales come from being in the right place at the right time. I'm amazed at how many times I call people and they say, 'I was just thinking about calling you'. The thing is, they never do if you don't call first. It's worse when you call and they say 'If only you'd called last week, we've just bought something'.

Try to make this work in your favour. Look to see if there are peak times in the day, year or month when people most want to buy from you, and go hell for leather then.

Work out your numbers: Your job with sales is not always to be winning work, but it is to be moving people down your sales funnel. Work out what your ratio of success is. This will vary from business to business, but I'll give you mine:

- One out of seven calls I make gives me a lead, or a meeting.
- One out of four leads gives me a chance to quote.
- We win one out of three jobs we quote for.

Therefore, each week, I work from a sales form which tells me how many calls I need to make, or how much work I need to bring in that week, or quote for.

The point of this is not to worry if work is not automatically coming in – so long as you are filling up your funnel with water, it will start to come out of the other end eventually.

Every week you will have a target. Once you have met your target, give yourself a break – you don't have to do any more for the rest of the week. Perhaps you've won a piece of work, or got some leads. Other weeks, you won't win any work, but will be keeping up your call level.

 Toolkit: **On the website there is a sales funnel template for you to work with (www.fromacorns.com).**

And sometimes something spooky happens. I will have had a week of really busting my guts and getting nowhere. Then, at the end of the week, out of the blue, someone calls us with a totally unrelated piece of work. I think of it as sales karma.

Grasp the nettle: The dread of making your calls is always worse than the reality. My advice is to plunge straight in. Make your hardest couple of calls first. After this, you should be on a roll, so do all your other calls quickly while the momentum is there. Once you've made your target, have a break and feel very smug.

Reward yourself: Most professional sales outfits award sales bonuses, since we are simple creatures and respond well to simple rewards. You should do the same for yourself. This can be either a pure cash bonus, or something else you've promised yourself like a CD, bottle of wine, or electronic gadget (my personal favourite).

Keep the bonuses to yourself. While a bit of strutting around after a sale is to be expected, coming in to work the next day on a new Harley-Davidson has a tendency to put other people's backs up.

Should you get someone else to do the dirty work?

"I'm not a sales person – should I get someone to sell for me?"
(Anika, Italian shoe designer)

I really felt for her when Anika explained her situation to me. She is a top designer, having designed shoes for Armani and Versace. She had some fantastic designs she knew would sell, so she set up in business. But a year and a half down the line she has no sales, and she's wondering if she should pack it all in. She simply can't face selling.

Sadly, Anika's problem is a common one. I think it's uniquely hard for 'creatives', as someone saying 'no' to them in a sales call is probably going to upset them more than, say, a cooker cleaning business.

My first piece of advice is to bite the bullet, and have one last push at selling. Work out your ratios so you know it's a numbers game. And just try to get in front of a few of the buyers, as I'm sure when you do, your natural enthusiasm will shine through.

The second option, finding someone else, will be hard. Using sales agents isn't always ideal as they won't necessarily put the passion into your product that you would. Chapter 22 on staff includes a section on recruiting sales staff, but it's hard for the start-up: you might not have enough cash to pay them, and you might not know enough about the job to know what to look for in a recruit.

A third option, which I've seen people do, is find a friendly sales person who'll do it for you part-time. Even if they give you a morning every few weeks, you can sit and watch them make appointments and learn how they do it. You can take turns to make calls (misery likes company!). These people don't necessarily have to come on the meetings they've set up. But you'll see that the inevitable knock-backs are not the end of the world.

Making a sales call

Get the right person (not the nice person): The first step is to make sure you are speaking to the person who will ultimately make the decision to buy. This can be harder than it sounds.

Imagine you have no purchasing power in your personal relationship (I know I don't). First, you might not actually realise this, and second, you are not going to admit this to a stranger on the phone.

Sales calls are scary, and sometimes the temptation is to just call people you like and are nice to you. There is nothing worse than spending months building a relationship with someone who you belatedly find out has nothing to do with the purchasing decision.

To find out if you have got the right person, you might just have to be blunt. Ask them outright who will make the final decision, and whether it is worth speaking to them as well.

> ### ♟ Entrepreneur's Secret: Get past the gatekeeper
>
> Many companies try very hard to keep people like you and me at bay. Often the gatekeeper will be a secretary. We once even had someone put on a funny voice pretending not to be themselves. Try the following:
>
> - The best way past them is with a referral. Get the name of anyone else in their department and say, 'Bob suggested I speak to them'.
> - To get put through – just give out your Christian name.
> - Don't be fobbed off with leaving a number and expecting them to call back – they hardly ever do.
> - Bear in mind that most purchasing decisions in big companies are not made by people at the top – perhaps you should aim a bit lower?
> - If there are no numbers on a big company's website, call the press office. They're usually friendly types not afraid of the phone, and will put you through.

Be clear about your objective from the call: No one likes a pushy sales person who tries to take you from an awareness of their product to giving out your credit card details in one five-minute call. Keep in mind AIDA (see page 111). Your first call can simply be to find out who has purchasing responsibility. If you get hold of the right person, then you can do a brief fact-find before sending them some information on your business. It will then probably take a further call for a meeting, or even to close the sale.

"Should you send a letter first or call?" (Rebecca, marketing)

In my experience, unless it's a very eye-catching letter, people will ignore it. I'd call first to find the right person and do an initial fact-find. Then I'd send them a letter. Chances are they won't read it, but then it gives you an excuse to call back. They'll feel guilty they haven't read it, and this gives you a good opportunity to push for a meeting. It also means they can't fob you off with 'Could you put something in writing to me?' which is a classic way of getting out of a call.

Face-to-face selling

Despite the promises of technology, most sales still need to be done face to face.

In a sales meeting, remember:

 Your objective is not to talk people into buying something. It is to get them to talk themselves into buying it

To find out what they want, you are going to have to question. As a rule of thumb, you should not talk more than 50 per cent of the time.

This is very hard for someone enthusiastic. Imagine going on a first date and the person spouts endlessly about themselves – it'll be a lonely taxi ride home for them. Instead, model yourself on Leslie Phillips and purr seductively, 'So pussy cat, tell me about yourself . . .'

1. Introduction

You should start by establishing your 'bona fides'. If a complete stranger came up to you in a bar and started an interrogation, you might be a tad cagey. A simple start might be: 'We have worked with X in your industry, won these awards, and have some great ideas of how we might be able to help you. However, before we do this, I need to know something about you.'

2. Fact-find

You need them to open up about their business, and what possible needs they have. To do this, you need to ask open-ended questions that get them talking, and not 'closed' ones that can be answered with just yes or no and so end your meeting:

Bad closed questions	Good open questions
Have you ever thought about . . .? ('No')	**What are** your main objectives?
How many products do you have? ('Six')	**Why** do you focus on this?
Do you buy from sales people? ('No, goodbye')	**How do** you choose a supplier?

> **⚓ Entrepreneur's Secret: Find out the hidden agenda**
> The answers people give you initially are not necessarily the real answers. Every brief we get asks for 'creativity'. However, the buyer's greatest concern is usually their mortgage. What they often mean is 'Give me something that is 99 per cent the same, but with a little twist'.

3. Present your benefits

At school, did you ever notice that if you directly quoted back to a teacher something they had previously said, your grades went up?

Your prospect should have just told you exactly what they want from a supplier. It is now a matter of you repeating back, 'It's funny you should say that using a local company is important, I used to go to school up the road' etc.

Don't worry if this seems completely transparent and disingenuous. The wonderful thing about flattery is, no matter how transparent it is – we still love it!

4. Handle their objections

You now want to find out what are your prospect's problems with you.

As odd as it may sound, objections are good. Think back to your last big purchase – I bet before you took the plunge there were lots of things you wanted to ask and check up on. It shows you are serious about making a purchase, and just want some reassurance. If you can successfully answer your prospect's objections, they will have to give you the work.

The three typical customer objections you will have to handle are:

1. loyalty to an existing supplier
2. lack of perceived demand
3. price.

 Toolkit: **The following table shows how you should handle objections.**

The customer says	What they mean	What you say
I'm happy with my current supplier	Loyalty	1. Don't slag the competition – you will undermine the person you are selling to. 2. Ask lots of questions about the competitor's service/product. 3. Stress the difference of your offer. 4. Get them to consider a trial offer.
I can't see me needing that	Demand	1. Actively question them about why not. 2. Talk through your current customer base and why they use you. 3. Come back to them.
It's too expensive	Price	1. Question the client – 'What makes you say that?' 2. Get comparisons with other products. 3. Question them on the benefits you offer and their need. 4. Stress the value you add and not the cost.

Remember:
- Don't go overboard with answers, and dig yourself into a hole. Answer succinctly and learn to shut up.
- Don't say, 'No, don't be a fool'. Nod sagely and say, 'It's interesting you should say that, what we found in fact was ...'
- Don't rubbish the competitors – it belittles you, and belittles the buyer. (Do, however, be sure to be patronising about them at *every* opportunity!)

5. Close the sale

I used to think it was somehow rude to ask for business. I would have fantastic meetings and practically become life-long buddies with my prospective clients, but never actually ask them for the business.

The simplest way is to wait until they have run out of objections, and then ask: 'Can we have your business?'

This may sound incredibly stupid, but like many stupid things it can work very well. Quite often, the person will be surprised, and say, 'Yes, OK then'. If not, at least they will tell you what other objections they have, which you can then counter.

> **⚓ Entrepreneur's Secret: Don't be afraid of silence**
>
> If you are dealing with a professional buyer, they will often have been trained to use silence as a way of intimidating you into dropping your price. Be prepared to shut up. Repeat a rhyme in your head if it helps (though try not to let your lips move at the same time as this can be a bit disconcerting). I have heard of two professional salespeople who sat silently looking at each other for a couple of minutes before one of them blinked. They're probably still there today.

It doesn't count unless it's written in ink

By closing the sale, I actually mean having a signed piece of paper in your hand. You might have a beautiful relationship with your client, built on trust and openness that transcends grubby contracts. And then they leave the company. As verbal agreements 'aren't worth the paper they're written on', you need confirmation from your customer, even if it's a confirmation email, or a signed piece of paper.

You have to do this quickly. The moment you walk out of the door, your relationship is already fading. A week down the line and you'll be a distant memory (and they certainly won't sign anything).

6. Beware of slack chat

You've closed the sale, you are on your way out. Don't blow it all by some random comments as you walk out of the door.

> *I had sold someone an insert into one of our magazines. At the end of the call I said, 'Err ... well, I look forward to inserting it for you' and hung up. There was a deathly hush around me as my colleagues stopped their work and looked up at me openmouthed.*

CHAPTER 17

How to win pitches

How to win pitches

Business, like battle, can be described by hours of waiting and routine punctuated by a few short moments of intense activity. Usually that activity is a pitch. Pitches are one of the few moments of life where huge consequences can rise from 25 minutes of heart-raising action (but fortunately not the only ones). It can be a pitch to raise finance, to win a major account, to convince a supplier or employee to join you. Or you might find yourself down on one knee pitching for something far more important (a word of warning from my painful experience – never do this if the object of your marriage proposal is on a swing at the time).

What staggers me is that people leave these moments to chance. Perhaps they think the pitch is just a rubber-stamping exercise where nothing is decided, or that their innate quality will shine through regardless. So they leave their fate in the lap of the gods. Nonsense. Victory goes to those who work hardest.

Numerous surveys and research exercises have revealed the same thing. Pitches are not decided on facts and prices. What wins pitches is personal relationships, chemistry and emotions.

Witness the bid for the 2012 Olympics:

Prior to the final presentations, the French had it in the bag. They had the best infrastructure and proposals, and there was a consensus that 'it was their turn'. Their presentation was an exercise in Gallic cool. They had a black-and-white film by film-maker Jean-Luc Besson, and a smooth speech by President Chirac.

The London team were the underdogs. So they took a single emotional theme – the legacy it would have for the children. They pitched to the hearts by getting the children to tell the story of what it would mean to them in their future. Apparently there were tears in the eyes of the committee members.

Those 40 minutes swung a $10 billion decision their way. Pitches are something we should definitely study.

There are three phases to the perfect pitch – two of which have nothing to do with the actual presentation.

Phase One: Foreplay

The diagnosis: Most pitches are won or lost long before you enter the room. You are there to offer a perfect solution, but how can you do that without knowing what the problem is?

The trick is to realise that the answer will not often lie in the pitch document or stated criteria. You have to discover their emotional need. Do they want the most exciting solution, or do they just want to pay the mortgage? Who will actually be making the decision, and how will they score it?

> *While other teams went for excitement, the Camelot team won the UK Lottery bid by playing safe. They realised the greatest worry for the civil servants running the pitch was they would be made to look stupid. So everything in their pitch was about reassurance.*
>
> *The London Olympic team realised the deepest worry of the Olympics committee was that the Olympics would leave no lasting impact. So they pitched one idea – legacy.*

Of course, the prospect may not tell you automatically, or even realise themselves what their need is. So you have to quiz them. Listen carefully to the subtext of their answers. Ask them to rank their priorities, get them to describe what a successful outcome in their minds would look like. Check your assumptions with them.

Then build your proposal around this as much as answering the stated criteria.

The warm-up: Most pitches are about building rapport. You should therefore use as many chances as you can to communicate and interact with the pitchee prior to the pitch to build this. Send muffins:

> *A small mailing house were pitching to one of the world's largest banks. A week before the pitch, the guy sent a box of muffins to the prospect. Three days before, he called to confirm and say how much he was looking forward to it. Unfortunately, the day before, the prospect found out they could only use their 'approved' supplier. But she liked the guy by now, and felt too guilty to cancel, so the pitch went as planned. Three days later she got her proposal from the approved supplier – it was outrageous. So she went with the small guy, and he built a huge contract off the back of it – and a box of muffins.*

Phase Two: The action

What order should you pitch? If the prospect is seeing a number of candidates, you don't want to be first on the list. It will all be too new for them to make a decision. Ideally you want to be second, by which time they're warmed up. Try not to go in after lunch, or they'll be asleep. And don't be last, as they'll be on information overload.

> *I once did a pitch to an Enterprise Agency at 5.00 p.m. on a Friday. One person on the panel started writing his Christmas cards in the middle of my pitch.*

The 'glide in': Try to have a relaxed chat as you enter. Be nice to the secretary.

Have a prepared question as you set up. The Queen apparently always asks 'Have you come far?' I ask, 'So, how's business at the moment?' Don't make it too personal. I heard about a sales person who said 'Did you see the football last night?' only to end up in a flaming argument before the meeting had kicked off.

Position the room the way you want it, and be prepared to move the panel around. Ideally, you don't want to sit directly opposite them – you want to be physically on 'the same side'.

The presentation: Thank them for inviting you and say how excited you are. Tell them what you are going to tell them, and how long it will take.

You then want to open up with an explanation of their problem. Don't skimp. This demonstrates both that you understand the client, and makes them realise they *really* need your solution.

You'll be lucky if people remember more than two things from your presentation, so don't overload it with facts and densely worded PowerPoint slides. Instead, think of the pitch as the chance to tell a simple story, based around their emotional needs. Your slides should run as a storyboard for this narrative.

Look for examples and illustrations. The Shell story at the start of the book illustrated my point far more powerfully than any description I could write.

If you want to pitch them something really adventurous, first give the client a safe option. You'll then be on safe ground, as they know you can work with them. Then you can move to the really exciting option. The risk otherwise is that they ditch you just because of some small risk in your big proposal.

Try to build rapport: You don't want this to be a slick presentation. The best pitches are ones that break down in the middle into a conversation and informal discussion with the client. So try to introduce deliberate breaks if you can. If you are showing something creative, give them two choices and get into a discussion about which one they like. The nirvana of pitches is when you are sitting together jointly constructing the ideal solution which the client will then see as their own.

Don't get into a slagging match. It sounds obvious, but in proving your point you will lose the larger battle. See the 'Objection handling' toolkit on pages 123–4.

Talk like a member of the client's team: the feeling created during the pitch should be one of a single team working together to discuss a solution. Clients want to know that you can be a part of their team. So speak as if you are sharing the problems: 'When we start the implementation ...'

Body language: When presenting to a large group, there are a few common mistakes to avoid:

- The 'anchor leg': The presenter seems to have one foot nailed to floor, so they wander round this one fixed point. If you are going to move, do it properly.
- The 'pocket rustler': Trust me – there is nothing more alarming than a presenter who keeps a hand in the pocket fiddling with change, or god knows what. Just don't go there.
- The 'noddies': It's very easy when doing a presentation only to look at the person who is nodding and smiling. Don't assume they're doing this because they like you (they might just be bursting for a pee). In my experience, the ones who give the least away in a pitch are the ones with the real power. So make sure you look them all in the eye in turn. Politicians are taught that if presenting to a large audience to look in a W or V shape – back left, front middle, back right in rotation. Everyone will think you are delivering a personal message just to them.

Other than that, act natural. OK, that's a complete tautology, but it's important that your personality comes across. If you are naturally a retiring type, don't try and act like Anthony Robbins or you'll come across like David Brent.

Summary: You've made your point, but it's worth concluding with a brief summary of your three main benefits. If you are using PowerPoint, you might want then to leave up a last slide of raving testimonials.

You now want questions. If they don't have any, ask some of your own: 'What elements most appeal to you?' 'Are there any concerns you have about our solution?' You want any of their worries out on the table now so that you can address them. If you don't do it now, you won't get a chance to later. Find out what the decision-making process will be. If it's not a formal pitch, try to get a commitment to future joint action: 'So, we'll work up option two, and you'll book a meeting with your other team members'.

The 'glide out': Beware 'the Columbo moment' on the way out of the door. You'll be relaxing as you leave, and some negotiators are trained to ask a really important question at this stage. They spring on you 'So, is anyone else interested in your ideas?' to which you gush, 'Definitely not, you're the first. I can't tell you how relieved I am.'

Don't do anything stupid until you are at least 100 metres from the building. I heard of an agency that had won a global advertising account, and then lost it when they booked a taxi on the client's account to take them to the airport.

Phase Three: The morning after

There is still a chance to influence the pitch after it's happened. Don't sit and wait for the phone to ring – follow your meeting up with a polite call or email. I don't believe anyone lost the job for being eager and enthusiastic.

If you lose a pitch, swallow your pride and dial '999' – that is, call the client 9 days later, then 9 weeks and then 9 months. There is always a moment of nervousness after a big purchase. You still have your rapport to build on, and if your competitor is failing to deliver on any aspect of their promise, you'll have a great chance to step in.

"How do I stop a prospect nicking all the ideas from my presentation and proposal and going away and doing it themselves?" (Rebecca, marketing)

It's a good point. After all, you can put all the 'copyright' warnings you like over a proposal, but you're not going to take them to court if someone steals it.

This problem stems from the temptation to throw everything into your presentations including the kitchen sink. A better idea in your presentation is first to explain your 'unique process'. Then give the client one or two tantalising creative ideas that come out of your process. That way, they are excited by the ideas, but they realise they need your fantastic secret process (i.e. you!) to come up with enough ideas to be viable.

CHAPTER 18

Promotion: how to get more customers

Promotion: How to get more customers

OK, so you have your first customers. Before you rush out hunting for more, you need to put a three-point plan in place to nurture these customers so that they become the foundation of your business.

Step One: Keep your customers loyal

There is no point busting a gut winning new customers if your existing customers just walk out of the door. This is blindingly obvious, yet far too many companies, including multinationals, fall into this trap. Surveys show that the average company will lose 50 per cent of their customers every four years.

As well as repeat business, loyal customers have other benefits:

- They will often pay higher prices because they trust you (and you know how much you can get away with charging them!).
- It is easier to sell them additional things.
- They cost less to service – you know what they need, and they know what you supply.

There has been a lot of hype about so-called loyalty cards, points and schemes. This is hogwash. As a French loyalty expert said:

> *You cannot keep your lover loyal by giving them points, and then offering to double them if they stay until breakfast.*

As a result, the most frequent business flyers are 'loyal' to an average of four different airlines – they join all the schemes and get the points regardless.

Customer loyalty isn't rocket science – it's often just a matter of love and attention.

Show your customers the love

As management guru Tom Peters highlights from numerous pieces of research:

> Sixty per cent of customers who leave a supplier do so not because of price, or a better product, but simply because of a lack of care and attention from their old supplier.

Give your customers a call or visit on a regular basis (not just when a pitch is coming up) – even if it's just to see how they're getting on. Take them out for a meal if you can afford it (legendary networker Jeffrey Archer held champagne and shepherd's pie parties for his best contacts).

If you can't visit or call them all, do a mailing to them. Don't just use this to flog new products. Produce a simple newsletter. Fill it with advice that helps them (rather than just news about you). Make it personal. Send them a card on their birthday, and a bottle at Christmas.

And don't just think about the person at the top. The MD's secretary might be the most important person in the company for you!

⚓Entrepreneur's Secret: If you lose a customer, swallow your pride

I know from bitter personal experience that when you lose a customer its very tempting to start howling and throw all your toys out of the cot, but that doesn't change anything. Try to treat this as just a delayed opportunity.

- Find out why you lost out. Chances are, they'll feel a bit bad for saying 'no' to you, so they should be prepared to give you honest and constructive feedback on what you could do better next time.

- While they're still feeling bad, ask if there is any other work coming up or anyone else in the organisation you should speak to.
- Keep in touch with them. They are still a hot prospect for you – their current supplier might mess up.

Step Two: Sell more stuff to your loyal customers

 It is five times easier to sell to an existing client than it is to a new one

If you have sweated blood to get in with a new client – keep selling to them. Go back to them and sell them other products and services. Think laterally about what these services might be. They obviously liked you enough to buy it the first time, so there's no reason why they shouldn't continue to buy.

> *Alistair Rutherford co-founded Edinburgh Preserves originally selling chutney made from his grandmother's recipe. On the success of this, they produced over 20 different varieties of chutneys as well as mustards, relishes and pudding sauces to supermarkets around the UK. If you think this is a ridiculous number of chutneys – look at a Heinz ketchup bottle – it says 57 varieties on the side!*

Step Three: Build word-of-mouth marketing

Wouldn't it be great if people loved your business so much they told their friends, and their friends told their friends? It can and does happen, and should be something you should strive for in your business. Referrals are much more likely to lead to a sale because people trust their friends. For a masterclass in doing this, sign up for a Boden catalogue (**www.boden.co.uk**). Then watch how they cleverly personalise their marketing to you.

Referrals don't always happen automatically. The following steps can help build them:

- Ask for referrals. Make it a habit after you have delivered a good service for a customer to ask them if there are three other people they know who might be interested. You can either wait for them to pass on the good word, which is great (if it actually happens). Or a quicker method is to say, 'Is it OK if I talk to them and mention your name?'
- Let your customers know how valuable referrals are for you. Stress this in meetings, put it in your literature and on your website.
- Give people an incentive for referrals. You could be blunt and offer them a 10 per cent discount on their next purchase, or a bottle of bubbly. Quite often recognition is enough – phone them up and say, 'Thanks for the lead, it looks promising and means a big deal for us' – it will give them a lovely warm glow, and a greater willingness to refer in future.
- Try viral marketing. This horrible term comes from the internet, where people forward funny website links and emails. It's a good general principle however. Make it easy for people to refer you. Give people things they can pass on, such as a stock of cards, stickers, newsletters, brochures, or just a simple website address. Anything that makes it easy to say, 'Hold on, I've got her number here ...'.
- Identify your star referrers. Keep track of who is your best source of sales leads. They might not actually be a client – they could be a supplier, the head of a trade body, or your bank manager. Be nice to them!
- Keep in touch. How many times have you found yourself saying to someone, 'Funnily enough, I was talking to someone about this the other day'? Consider a newsletter or just regular updates on your progress.

> **⚓Entrepreneur's Secret: Encourage people to complain**
> You will probably have heard the saying that while a happy customer might tell one other person, an unhappy customer will tell around five others. But interestingly, research by a major bank found that the customers who complained the most were actually their most loyal customers. If you can resolve a problem with a customer to their satisfaction, they will trust you more in future, and will be more likely to tell others about the positive experience.
>
> So, get customers to give you their feedback. Have comment boxes for customers, and make the effort to ask people how happy they are with your product. Don't simply rely on them telling you, because they may just seethe in silence, and then spread the bad word.

Other promotion

OK, you have a bedrock of loyal customers who are spreading the good word, now you want to start filling up the funnel with some more leads.

Direct marketing: This has got a bad name. The problem is that you are often trying to get from Awareness to Action (see page 111) in one move. Even the largest companies typically only get a response rate of 1–2 per cent. If you are lucky, the other 98 per cent either don't see your mailer or just ignore it and won't get upset with you bombarding them with junk mail.

In direct marketing, a personal touch can make all the difference

If you are going to do direct marketing, then here are some tips:

- Follow up your mailing with a call. Remember AIDA? Your hit rate will go up considerably if you call people to see what they thought of your offer.
- Make sure your database is good. If possible, do a quick call first to check the contact details are right. While you are at it, why not ask if they are the right person to send information to – you will already be two steps up your sales funnel.

- Do a trial run with a limited number first, and get someone external to your business to proofread it for the glaring mistakes that are so easy to miss.

  A marketing company was running a campaign targeting wealthy investors. A temp in the office had been playing around with the system, but no one did a test of the campaign before sending the letters off. The envelopes were fine, it's just that they all contained a letter which started 'Dear capitalist bastard'.

- Make it different. This is the golden rule we keep coming back to. It's a noisy world out there, and if you want to get noticed, you've got to stand out from the crowd. Don't, however, follow the example of one company who recently stuck thousands of flyers designed to look like parking tickets under car windscreen wipers – doh!

Your website: In my first edition of this book, I was perhaps a little sceptical about websites, saying that people put too much faith in them doing all their sales work for them.

  "When you next update your book you need to push the internet more. You say only have a website if you need one, but who doesn't these days? When at work, if there's anything I'm looking for I look on the internet, using Google. If you provide a service I need but don't have a web presence, I'm not likely to know about you.

  Besides we get most of our business (we're a word processing service) from our website and it could easily give you business in areas you never expected to trade. We're based in Sussex, England, our furthest client is in Western Australia."

  (Ashley, word processing)

OK, I hold my hands up in apology! It's possibly because I spent a week living off the internet once that I have a misplaced scepticism. But I also know a great 3D design company (www.web3D.co.uk) who get a huge volume of their work from the internet.

So, you must have one!

However, don't think that once you have a website the job is done. You have to get people to visit your store. Spend some time optimising your website so that it appears on the search engines. Consider reciprocal links with other sites, or perhaps banner advertising.

You could also consider an email newsletter. Again, make sure what you have to say adds value to your contacts. Not many of them will really care about your news, but if you can inform, educate and entertain them on a topic they are interested in, then they're less likely to put you in their junk email list.

A four-piece guitar band from Liverpool you say? Nah, it'll never catch on . . .

PR: Getting a mention in the press can be valuable. It is probably cheaper than advertising, and can give your new business more credibility. It can also build the good buzz around you, and reassure customers. Vitally, it can also be hugely satisfying to the old ego (unless it is under the 'Court Appearances' section).

To get a mention in the press, remember that journalists are human (despite what some people might tell you), so:

- Make your story compelling. If your news does not look eye-catching in the first five seconds, then it's unlikely to get covered.
- Don't rely on blanket press releases. As with every type of selling, there is no replacement for picking up the phone and calling them directly to discuss your release before sending it to them. Then follow it up afterwards.
- The press wants to see a small business do well, particularly up against a big company. Don't play down the emotions of your story.
- If you've got a sympathetic contact, nurture them. Keep them posted with your good news, and if they run a good story – send them a bottle of wine as a thank-you.

> An employee from a small charity took a journalist from one of the national papers out for a boozy lunch. Over the next year, he ran six half-page spreads on the charity's work. An initial outlay of £55 brought in tens of thousands of pounds of good publicity.

- Try the picture desk as well. Sometimes a good photograph can get you much more coverage.

  A friend won a contract to do the plants and flowers for a large department store. None of the press covered this. However, then a family of birds made a nest in the middle of her big display. The photos of this got her great coverage!

 Toolkit: Visit the website for a sheet of advice on writing a good press release: www.fromacorns.com.

Advertising: We live in a world of noise:

- It is estimated that the average consumer sees about 1 million marketing messages a year.
- Last year in the USA $100 billion was spent on direct marketing. A 1 per cent response rate is good – 2 per cent will usually get a marketer a promotion.
- Google currently searches over 3 billion websites.
- A typical modern household has access to 32 TV channels.
- There are over 1,000 business and professional magazines and newsletters in the UK.

And yet, a man recently sold his forehead as advertising space on eBay. He got $30,000 for one month.

My point is this: advertising is an easy way to blow a lot of money very quickly for very little result. If you are going to do it, follow the following tips:

- Remember AIDA: People won't buy your product/service the first time they hear about it. Don't rely on just one advert, but make sure you have a campaign that will reach your target a number of times, and is backed up by lots of other selling and promotion.
- Be different: You cannot buy yourself attention, but you can do it by being creative. One of the best examples is the vans that Innocent Smoothies use. They're covered in grass and have horns on the front. This builds word of mouth, and sticks in the mind – and that's what counts.
- Make them think: Ideally, rather than just interesting your prospects, a good piece of advertising will *intrigue* them. You are

then much closer to a sale. Being eye-catching and funny doesn't require a huge spend on advertising.

I recently saw a leather coat store with the sign: 'Due to an expensive divorce, Mr Toskana is having to sell his stock fast'. The cost of the sign must be a few pounds, but it is seen, and probably remembered, by thousands of people each day.

> ⚓ **Entrepreneur's Secret: Don't be talked into taking advertising by good salespeople**
> Make sure you have a plan and stick to it. To illustrate my point – how do these people sell advertising space to punters? Do they stick ads in magazines hoping you'll read them? Of course they don't. They pick up the phone and call you.

Networking v. notworking: Networking is the fine art of mingling with prospective customers at an event or golf course, to get work from them. For this reason it is also known as notworking.

Done well, and with the right people, you can move a person the whole way from awareness to action in the course of a five-minute chat. There are many forums where you can meet prospects: Chambers of Commerce, local business clubs, industry forums.

However, before attending each one, carefully consider whether you will actually meet many of your potential customers there.

Marketing Judo
Building your business using brains not budget

John Barnes &
Richard Richardson

Partnering: There is a fantastic book called *Marketing Judo* by the team who took a local fish and chip restaurant, Harry Ramsden's, into a global brand. Their philosophy is that small nimble companies can achieve huge success by partnering with large established businesses.

There are many different ways you can do this:
• It could be by enticing a local celebrity to eat in your restaurant, giving you excellent publicity, in return for perhaps one free meal.

- You can do it on a small scale. For example, a local sports team might promote your sports shop if you provide them with free shirts.
- Alternatively you can do it on a huge scale.

> *My wife used to babysit a small boy called Richard Tait. When he grew up he invented a new board game called Cranium. However, his business only had four staff, and he didn't have the clout to get into the big toy retailers. But he did have a contact at Starbucks. They were looking for other items to sell which could complement their brand. They took Cranium on, first locally, and then nationally. It became, after café lattes, one of their fastest selling items. Then one night on the* Oprah Winfrey Show, *Julia Roberts mentioned how she loved playing the game. Cranium went on to sell 11 million copies, making it the fastest selling independent board game in history.*

CHAPTER 19

Keeping hold of your cash

Keeping hold of your cash

Cash is king

By now, your business is up and running, and you are making profits. It's time to have a check on your cash position.

There is a big difference between profits and cashflow. There are too many heartbreaking examples of fantastic businesses who have great products, good profits and customers lined up, but go bust simply because they don't have enough cash in the bank for a short period.

You'll hear this many times as you start up, but it doesn't make it any less true:

Turnover is vanity, profit is sanity, cash is reality.

Your cash can get eaten up by customers not paying in time (or at all), too much stock, or too much spending on equipment and overheads. Ironically, it is often businesses that are growing fastest who are at most risk from this problem – technically known as 'overtrading'.

Good cashflow will not make your business a success, but one thing is sure:

 Poor cashflow can break your business almost faster than anything else

So how do you stop this happening to you?

The ten golden commandments of getting paid

You have to learn to watch your cash like a hawk. Unfortunately, there are quite a few dodgy business people out there, and they can play havoc with a new-start business. Remember, if something sounds too good to be true, it probably is.

> **Until that money is in the bank (*and* the cheque has cleared), you haven't sold anything**

1. **Open your bank statements:** At every stage of your business, you should have a strong sense of how much cash you have in the bank and what the next month will look like. Don't stick your head in the sand and try to ignore this. Of course, you need proper books (which we are coming to), but your cash position should always be at the back of your mind.

2. **Hire a dragon:** It must be someone's clear responsibility in the business to chase up your overdue accounts, and you need a system for doing this. If there is only you, make sure you set aside a regular time each month to do this. Consider getting a book-keeper (see the next chapter) to do this, or an outside agency – see below.

3. **Don't automatically give credit:**

   When I produced my first yearbook, I was a penniless student but turned up to pick up the book from the printers with the cash in my briefcase. Strangely, nobody asked me for the money, and I kept my mouth shut. They automatically gave me thirty days' credit. I couldn't believe it. They were oblivious to the financial risk of a 20-year old student with a thirst and £800 in used twenties. I made a mental note to myself not to extend credit to my customers unless I absolutely had to.

   Giving credit to people is exactly the same as lending them money. Just think how many new clients you would be happy to do this for. In fact, think about how many friends and members of your family you'd do this for!

4. **Beware new clients:** If a new client demands credit, and you are nervous about them:
   - Ask them for some trade references and check them out. If they cannot provide them, that should raise some questions.
   - Ask them for a deposit or a first stage payment for work in progress. That usually sorts out the time-wasters.
   - Don't place large orders with suppliers on behalf of new customers. Their non-payment can put you out of business at a stroke. Let them place the order directly with the supplier. You can always convince them of the discount they will get by going direct. In the longer term, you can do this for them.

5. **Invoice in stages:** If you deliver a service or product that takes a while to complete, invoice in stages from the start of the job. Our terms are a third on commencement of the job, a third on sign-off and a third on delivery. This greatly improves cash-flow.

6. **Negotiate:** Negotiate payment terms with as much gusto as you negotiate price:

   A business owner was selling to a big supermarket. After they had shaken on the deal, and he was packing up his bags, they brought up payment. Their standard terms were to pay in 90 days. If they were to pay in 30 days, they would charge him 10 per cent of the cost. Imagine that – charging someone to pay them! That has got to be good.

7. **Don't wait:** Old debts are harder to collect, so don't wait 90 days before chasing overdue bills. As soon as an invoice is past your credit terms, institute your credit control procedure:

8. **Develop pester power:** Learn a lesson from toddlers – the person shouting loudest will get served first. Many of your customers may operate a policy of not paying until shouted at. This is illuminated by Lord Heseltine in his early days in business:

> *We instituted a system of three levels for paying debtors: (1) those from whom solicitors' letters had been received; (2) those from whom a writ had been received; (3) those from whom a writ had been received 14 days ago. My first piece of advice in dealing with creditors is to pay the latter first.*

And he was the former Minister for Trade and Industry!
You should have a procedure similar to the following:

1. Phone up. Ask the person politely when you can expect payment (quite often they will have been waiting for a call before authorising payment). Often, they will fob you off ('It's in the post', 'Our cheque run is next week'). In which case:

2. Keep them at their word. If they said five days, phone back then and ask where it is. Keep doing this until they keep their word. If you get no progress then:

3. Send a 'seven-day letter'. A lawyer or debt collection firm will be able to do this for a small sum. They will send a legal letter hinting at dark consequences if you don't pay within seven days. This acts as a very persuasive memory jogger!

4. If they are still not paying, you can seek recourse to lawyers or the small claims court. However, at this stage you have to be honest with yourself whether they are ever going to pay. You could spend a large amount of time and money in an attempt to salve your pride. Better sometimes just to chalk it up to experience, and tighten your credit policy.

Some companies have turned pestering into an art form. A big London advertising agency sends a scruffy, smelly and frankly menacing courier round to sit in the plush reception area of their clients until he is handed a cheque.

Be prepared to use unorthodox methods to get people to pay

Or, my personal favourite, you could engage the services of the Payment Chicken (**www.paymentchicken.com**). According to its website, the 6-foot day-glo chicken will follow around your debtors until they come forth with the readies. ('At no time will the chicken be anything but well behaved' it adds sweetly.)

9. **Don't rely on regulation:** There are now well-meaning regulations allowing you to charge interest on late payment of bills, and many people put this on their invoices. I haven't heard of a single person who has made this stick. Are you prepared to take your customer to court over this? If they aren't going to pay you, then this clause is unlikely to help.

10. **Consider invoice discounting/factoring:** This involves signing over all your invoices to someone (usually the bank) for them to chase up. They pay you an immediate amount, and then the balance – minus their commission – when the bill is settled. This used to be a sign of a company in trouble, but it now has a much better image, and a much politer approach to collecting amounts. Some of our suppliers use this, and I think it is a sign of good management.

And, while you're at it ...

Join the club: This is terrible to say, but you don't want to be great at paying your suppliers if no one is paying you. So, with the following provisos, institute a policy of not paying until you have been paid.

A foundry business was experiencing a tight cash squeeze. The MD told his book-keeper to write out 63 cheques for all his creditors, but to lock them in a safe until they phoned up for payment. A couple of months later, his position was better, and he asked the book-keeper about the cheques. Fifty-seven were still in the safe.

The provisos are:
- Always pay individuals and your smallest suppliers on time. Possibly, like you, this is their only income. If you don't pay them – they won't eat.
- Always pay your key suppliers promptly. You want a good working relationship with them. If you never pay them, they're not going to pull out the stops to do a good job for you.
- If you've got good cash in the bank – pay your bills promptly.

CHAPTER 20

Aunty Nan's guide to keeping your books

Aunty Nan's guide to keeping your books

Most entrepreneurs are terrible at keeping track of their finances. Good entrepreneurship is about starting new ideas, big-picture stuff. Good book-keeping is about fine detail, and making sure everything tallies.

But you need both in a business. While well-kept accounts will not make you a success, giving them little or no attention can bring down an otherwise successful business.

We were very lucky in our early days to find a brilliant book-keeper – Aunty Nan – who has been keeping books all her life. This section is put together in the simplest way possible with her canny advice.

I strongly recommend that you employ a book-keeper. It needn't cost the earth – as little as £6 an hour for a couple of hours a week. It may seem like a cost in the short term but in terms of the time it will save you, and the peace of mind from knowing everything is in order, is well worth it.

However, it is still important that you learn the fundamentals of keeping your books.

Basic book-keeping

The golden rule when setting up a system is that it should be simple and methodical.

Do I need a software package? There is no reason why you shouldn't do your books by hand with a simple accounts book. However, there is a range of simple software packages that can help. I used QuickBooks and Sage Instant. Don't go for anything more advanced unless you really need to. It will be easy to upgrade your system as time goes on.

Step One: Keep a record/invoice of each sale

You need to keep an invoice or a receipt for everything you sell. This should include your address, the date and your VAT number (if you are registered for VAT).

File these in a ring-bound file in numerical order. When something is paid, write 'paid' at the top, and the date and cheque number. You will need a new file for every year.

Step Two: Keep a receipt of everything you purchase

Keep receipts for everything you buy. And I mean everything – parking tickets, petrol receipts, cups of tea, magazines, newspapers, etc.

Make sure you ask for a VAT receipt (i.e. one that shows the VAT number). Many places such as restaurants and petrol stations don't automatically give them. A credit card receipt is not a VAT receipt.

Put a number on every receipt (in the order you received them). Put these in a file called 'Purchases'.

Not everything can be claimed back against tax. See the next chapter on tax for a rough idea of what you can and cannot claim. However, my accountant's advice is:

> **⚒ Entrepreneur's Secret: Make a claim**
> If in doubt, claim for it.

Step Three: Enter these in your records book

Enter the details of your sales and purchases in your records book.

For your sales, you need to record:
- the date
- the sale or invoice number
- the customer name
- the amount (including VAT).

If you are registered for VAT, you will also need to include the amount of VAT, and the total without it.

For your purchases, record:
- the date received
- the name of the supplier
- the number you've given it
- the amount (including VAT).

If you are registered for VAT, you will also need to note the amount of VAT, and the total without it.

The next columns detail the nature of what you purchased. You can make these up depending on your most common purchases. Typically, you might include a brief breakdown of your direct supplies, and your overheads.

Step Four: Reconcile your statements

Now comes the really fun bit. You have to go through all your bank statements every month and check that the reality of what has come in and out of your account actually matches your beautiful books. This is important as it is the one time you can catch any glaring mistakes in your book-keeping.

Every cheque you have written, or payment you have made has to be accounted for. If there is a payment from your account that you don't have a receipt for, you have to make a note of this in your books.

Cash in hand

While obviously lovely to hold, real-life cash actually makes your books a bit fiddly. It's harder to track, and the temptation for it to mysteriously end up in your back pocket without touching your accounts is very high. Not surprisingly, tax inspectors are very alert to this. They know the types of businesses where this is most prevalent, and the types of purchases where it will happen. They will therefore go through your accounts with a fine toothcomb looking for evidence of this.

One solution is to use a credit card for your business expenses.

An alternative is to have a petty cash box. You can use this to pay for small purchases *providing* you keep a clear record of what you put in and take out of this box. The emphasis is from Nan, and I can tell you, if our petty cash box is out by 50p, it's like the Spanish Inquisition in our office.

Using an accountant

Ideally, a good accountant should save you more money than they cost. This depends partly on finding a good accountant, but perhaps more so on using your accountant in the right way.

The following are some of the wrong ways to use an accountant:

✗ Don't get an accountant to do all your day-to-day book-keeping for you. A good book-keeper will be far cheaper (an accountant should be able to recommend one).

✗ Don't turn up at the end of the year with a big shoe-box full of hundreds of dog-eared bits of paper you have been filing under the bed. They will possibly be able to make some semblance of order from this, but it's unlikely to be 100 per cent accurate, and it will be very expensive.

✗ Don't get your accountant to produce your business plan for you. It is vital you 'own' and understand everything in your plan. If necessary, get some help with more complex financial aspects – but it has to be *your* plan.

✗ Don't try to do everything and complete all your year-end tax, allowances, depreciation and so on. Well, OK, you can, but it's unlikely you will get it all right. And hey, life's too short and it's sunny outside.

✗ Don't just speak to them when things are too late. Seek their knowledge early on in your start-up process to get advice about what legal form your business should take, when you should pick your tax year, the types of expenses you should claim and so on.

It is far better that you keep methodical and simple records, and present them to the accountant at the end of the year for them to weave their special accountant's magic with them.

How to get a good accountant: The best way has to be a recommendation. Go along to business networking events and ask successful business people in similar types/sizes of business who they use. Alternatively, ask business support organisations, your bank manager or lawyer for a recommendation.

As they found out with Enron, you don't necessarily want your accountant to be very exciting and sexy (apologies, Gordon).

CHAPTER 21

Tax

Tax

I make no apologies for this being one of the shortest sections of the book. Apart from laziness, I have the following excuses:

- It's a fact of life. Some people get too obsessed with avoiding tax to the detriment of growing their business.

 Don't let the tax tail wag the business dog

- It's not going to make you successful.
- As soon as I write the details, they become out of date.

> *"There is an error in the tax section – cars have not been taxed on age, engine size (and mileage) since April 2002. Cars are now taxed on CO2 emissions, which is not necessarily the same as age/engine size." (David)*

It is important to understand the tax implications for your business, even if you get an accountant to complete your tax return. Don't worry, it makes my head bleed as well, but get a nice cup of tea and sit down. I'll try to make this as painless as possible.

This section is not an exhaustive guide to tax regulations. I'll give you nuggets of wisdom and point you in the direction of more detailed advice.

The Inland Revenue and Customs and Excise departments have now merged into HM Revenue and Customs (HMRC), so you only have one source to deal with. Generally they are very helpful and patient with people starting in business, so don't hesitate to give them a call on 0845 915 4515. They also have a clear guide on the tax issues for people starting in business. You can get it from **www.hmrc.gov.uk/startingup/index.htm**

Income tax

What you have to consider when starting out:

The legal form of your business: As we looked at on pages 78–9, you have to make a choice about the legal form your business will take. As well as all the other considerations, tax will play a part in your thinking.

- If you are a sole trader, then you are taxed as an individual – all the profits of the business are taxed in the same way as if this was a straight salary.
- With a limited company, your business is a separate legal entity. You will pay less tax on higher profits than you would as a sole trader. You can also take payment as dividends at a lower rate of tax. However, as an employee of the company you will have to pay normal tax on your salary. For this reason, some business people pay themselves a very low level of salary and take their income instead as regular dividend payments (providing the business makes sufficient profits).

Moving from employee to start-up: There are a number of factors you should consider as you move from employee to start-up.

If you make a loss in your first year of trading, you might be able to claim back tax you have paid in previous years as an employee.

You should also check to see if you qualify for any government tax credits. It's worth a bit of checking as there are some worthwhile schemes like childcare vouchers. Visit: **www.hmrc.gov.uk/menus/credits.htm**

Cashflow and tax: An unplanned for and unexpected tax bill can cripple a small business. You also don't want HMRC chasing you for payment, as they have serious powers. But there's no point whingeing about them – it is the fault of the business for not anticipating the bill.

It is a hard discipline to learn if you have been previously taxed at source as an employee. Get into the habit of putting money by throughout the year to pay your tax bill. You can also pay your tax in instalments throughout the year.

What you can and can't claim for: Ask your accountant for detailed advice about this, but here is a rule of thumb:

You can claim:

✓ some expenses if you are working from home (but only if these are 'additional expenses')
✓ business gifts (up to a limit), but not food and drink
✓ work travel
✓ subsistence (i.e. cost of food when away on work business)
✓ relevant books, magazines, newspapers (including the Sunday ones for all-important 'research')
✓ staff entertaining – up to a limit
✓ the cost of employing your wife or husband (if you can demonstrate the work they actually do, and you're paying them the going rate).

You cannot claim:

✗ your own income and living expenses
✗ client entertaining and meals
✗ travel to and from your place of work
✗ clothing, i.e. suits
✗ parking tickets and fines

I have known some people who have really turned this into an art. A friend put her top-of-the-range home hi-fi system through the business books as she claimed it was solely to play training DVDs for her staff. Another would once a year find that an essential work exhibition just happened to occur at holiday time, and in a warm sunny country, so of course he could put the trip, and associated essential fact-finding, through the business.

> *"My ultimate challenge is how to claim back first-class plane travel as 'essential business expenses', as coach class just doesn't quite cut it somehow." (Claire, jewellery designer)*

Claire, I like your style! If you want a chance for an upgrade, one approach that might work is to sign up for an airline loyalty card. However, before you try more direct methods I'd advise you to read the section on 'tax dodging' at the end of the chapter first.

⚑ **Entrepreneur's Secret: Expense claims**
Bear in mind, the official term is 'wholly and exclusively for business use'. Therefore, if you make a trip to see a friend, and do some business while there, it is unlikely you can claim the whole thing back.

Equipment: If you buy equipment for your business, you might not be able to claim back the total cost of this in the first year. Instead you may be able to claim tax relief in the form of 'capital allowances'. Ask HMRC for their help sheet IR206 on Capital Allowances, or download it from their website.

Cars and tax: Unfortunately this is one of the most complex areas of tax. Basically, the government is not keen on all of us fat cats swanning around in big German cars noising up the neighbours and polluting the environment.

If your business provides you with a car, you will find the tax on this is eye-watering. It is often far simpler to keep your car private, and pay all the repairs and insurance yourself. Then you can claim back the business mileage you do during the year. A typical mileage rate is 45p a mile. Over the course of the year, this should pay for itself.

Your first company car may not be quite what you anticipated

⚑ **Entrepreneur's Secret: Avoid flash cars**
You do not have to buy a flash car to impress clients:
- They will hardly ever see it. Mind you,

  I used to drive an old battered Renault 5, dubbed uncharitably by a friend, 'Bozo the Clown's car'. After one meeting, a client followed me out into the car park. I was horrified. I said good-bye, walked past the car, round the corner, and hid in a bush until he'd gone back into the office before nipping round and driving off.
- It will make them jealous and worry they are paying you too much.

  A great mission statement from a design agency: 'Macs not Mercs'.

VAT

If your annual turnover is over a certain limit (in 2007, £61,000), you generally have to be registered for VAT.

VAT is the tax on the value added at each stage of production. From the mining of the raw material for your product until it reaches the customer, this amount snowballs until the last person holding the parcel has to pay the amount. This is a clever trick of the government, as you are essentially acting as their tax collector.

The main problem with VAT used to be the paperwork and admin, but, all credit to them, the government are doing a lot to simplify this.

VAT bands: There are four classifications of VAT:

- the standard rate of VAT (currently 17.5 per cent)
- a special 5 per cent rate for unusual things
- zero-rated for VAT
- goods and services that are exempt from VAT.

Exempt-rated goods include things like selling and leasing property, insurance, post, some training and education services.

Zero-rated goods are essentially those things the government decide are 'good' for us. They include:

- food (but not 'bad' things like hot prepared food, catering or 'non-essentials' like confectionery)
- books and magazines (but not 'bad' ones that are full of ads).
- exports
- children's clothing.

The main difference between these two is that if you only deal in exempt goods, you cannot be VAT registered.

As you might imagine, actually defining what is 'good' and 'bad' is not clear cut, and is subject to a fair degree of legal wrangling.

There was a big expensive legal battle as the makers of Jaffa Cakes argued with the Inland Revenue that their products were 'cakes', so not liable for VAT, and not 'biscuits', which would have been liable for VAT.

The HMRC provides leaflets on this, and continual updates. If you are in any way unsure, phone them up and ask them (0845 010 9000). It's important to get this right as if on an inspection they find you have not been charging VAT on something you should have, they can demand back-dated payments – which will come direct from your profit.

Also, be careful about splitting down your service. If we gave a total price for producing and delivering a book, it would be zero-rated. If we charged extra for delivery, we would have to charge VAT on that.

The system

Generally, you will file a VAT return every quarter. You can opt to do it monthly if you are a masochist, anally retentive or are reclaiming tax. There are also a number of simplified VAT schemes for smaller businesses. These include:

- **Annual accounting:** Below a set turnover level, you can work out with the VAT people an estimated amount for the year, based on your previous year's return. You then pay this monthly by direct debit, with a balancing adjustment at the end of the year. You can adjust this throughout the year if circumstances change.
- **Cash accounting:** This can help cashflow as you only account for VAT on the cash you receive and pay out, rather than on invoices you issue and receive.
- **Flat rate scheme:** This very simply calculates VAT as a flat rate percentage of your turnover. The percentage depends on the sector you are in. However, you won't be able to reclaim any of the VAT you pay, as this is taken into consideration as part of the percentage calculation.
- **Retail schemes:** If you sell direct to the public you may find it difficult to issue a VAT invoice for each sale. There are several retail schemes available that may help.
- **Bad debt relief:** You can claim this if you don't get paid.

You have to keep your records for six years. If the VAT people are investigating you, they can look back three years.

For information on all these schemes, call the HMRC helpline 0845 010 9000.

If you make a mistake: The VAT people have tightened up their enforcement with a whole scale of statutory fines for late payment and errors. However, they have an obligation to go a bit easier on small businesses. If you are having problems, or have made a mistake, follow the cardinal rule of business: phone them up and tell them! They will be much more understanding if you admit to genuine problems than if they think you are trying to pull a fast one.

Tax dodging and cash in hand

There is a fine line between playing all the rules in your favour, and breaking them outright.

It is *very* tempting when you start out to treat all income as your own personal cash, and be less than scrupulous in what you report to the taxman. Be careful! I would avoid this for a number of reasons:

You'll get caught: The Revenue has been around for a lot longer than you have, and it is unlikely you will be the first person to have thought of your wizard wheeze for tax avoidance. Don't underestimate their ability to track you down.

During Wimbledon, local house owners started to rent out their drives as parking spaces. The Revenue got wise to this. Tax inspectors would walk up and down the street checking who was doing this, looking at adverts in newsagents and local newspapers and asking around. They then checked that the owners were reporting this income in their tax returns.

Similarly, if someone pays you as a freelance, you will need to account for this as it will be on your customers' records, and the Revenue will often follow the chain.

You do not want to come to the attention of the Revenue: An inspection can be a very time-consuming and expensive affair. Generally, this is helped by filing your return on time, paying promptly, and having figures that do not seem completely out of the ordinary (trust me – they know what a business such as yours should be declaring).

It is bad business practice: You need to be disciplined and think long term with your business. There is no point splashing out a large amount of cash one month and buying yourself some nice toys, only to find when things get tight a few months later you have no cash left and go bust. Get into the habit of paying yourself a regular salary, and bonuses when you make a big sale.

Also, the whole point of being self-employed and having money is to have freedom. If you have to spend the whole of your life stressing about your various fiddles and dodges, it defeats the whole purpose.

CHAPTER 22

Taking on staff

Taking on staff

So, your business is growing, you're making enough money for yourself, but getting overloaded with work. Is it time to hire staff?

Can you afford *not* to employ someone?

> *"Manufacturer, sales, PR, design, research, cat feeder. When, oh when can I employ someone else!? Never worked as hard and having an obscenely good time!" (Ruth, florist)*

Hiring your first employee is a big step for a small business. Typically, you will worry:

- it's expensive
- there's too much red tape
- I can't trust anyone to do the job as well as me.

Expense: Wages will represent a significant expenditure. Before committing to a full-time member of staff you should consider outsourcing, freelancers and part-timers. There are tax implications (National Insurance) on hiring staff, but they are not prohibitive, and no reason not to take someone on.

However, before you put off hiring someone:

Work out what your opportunity cost is

This is another useful lesson from economics:

Q: You are doing deliveries – a job that it would cost, say, £10 an hour to employ someone else to do. You are making an additional £10 an hour profit?

A: Wrong! Say your objective is to grow your business by £100,000. That works out as roughly £2,100 extra income a week, or £60 an hour. So every hour you are doing a task that will not significantly grow your business (e.g. book-keeping, filing, deliveries, manufacturing) you are in fact *losing* £50 an hour!

It may seem like a cost to you in the short term, but only by looking at the long term will you grow your business.

Red tape: The Government has a lamentable desire to tinker with regulations, which rarely makes a small business owner's life easier.

> *We were looking to recruit a sales manager. However, we were told that we could not use the word 'ambitious' in our job advert as that would constitute age discrimination. Un-be-lieve-able.*

However, if you are a reasonable and sensible employer, you should not have too much to worry about.

If you are worried about falling foul of the law, then I thoroughly recommend you become a member of the Federation of Small Businesses. For a reasonable annual fee, you get access to a free employment advice line (**www.fsb.org.uk** or telephone 01253 336000). We have saved a fortune in legal fees by using this (and we're supposed to be good at this whole business thing).

I can't trust anyone: The biggest reason people don't hire staff is a fear of letting go. You can see from Ruth's example at the start of the chapter, the reason she's doing all the jobs is that she doesn't want to delegate. That's fine if you want to stay small (though you should still consider the alternatives below), but short-sighted if you want to grow. The section on 'delegation' below shows some ways to tackle this fear.

Alternatives: outsourcing and freelancers

Before hiring a full-time member of staff, consider the more flexible alternatives.

Outsourcing certain jobs to specialists or freelancers can seem expensive. However, they will often bring a higher degree of expertise. You also must consider your 'opportunity cost' – i.e. how much more you could earn if you were out selling and not driving the delivery van.

The following are some of the areas small businesses can typically outsource:

- Deliveries: Unless delivery is a vital stage in strengthening the relationship with your customer, get someone to do it for you.
- Book-keeping: See Chapter 20.
- Manufacturing: This can seem a heretical question in a product business, but you must ask yourself – is my real talent in the physical manufacture of each product, or is it more in the originality of the design, packaging or promotion?

> *McClaggan Smith sell a range of popular china mugs. If you are drinking out of a humorous mug now, have a look at the bottom to see if their name is there.*
>
> *They used to employ staff to run a pottery kiln making these mugs. However, this gave them huge staff costs, and there were problems with seasonality, quality control and so on. Instead, they outsourced production to a specialist mug supplier and now just seal on the designs and package in-house. Their real talent as a company is spotting talented designers and their network of sales channels.*

What to look for in a member of staff

If you are ready to take the plunge, there are two golden rules in looking for an employee:

1. Hire for attitude not aptitude

It is scary taking on staff. As we saw in Chapter 12 on marketing, when faced with scary purchases people don't go for the best, they go for the *least worst*. Resist the following scenario:

> *You get a good gut feeling for someone in an interview, and are really impressed by their can-do attitude. However, they don't have much industry experience. Then an ex-employee from your competitors comes in. OK, they don't interview very well and are a bit lacklustre, but they've got good qualifications, and after all, your competitors hired them ...*

Don't do it! Trust your gut instinct.

Bear in mind, you can train most people in most skills fairly quickly. It is nigh on impossible to change someone's attitude. If they are grumpy and negative, they will spread this around your business and customers.

2. Resist hiring clones of yourself

> *"As an entrepreneur, I have a tendency to skip over the things that bore me, to focus on something new." (Al, training company)*

You definitely need starters and sales people, but you need an equal balance of finishers back in the office to deliver on the promises all your 'yes' people are making.

If you are a buzzy extrovert, it is no surprise that you are going to be tempted to hire other buzzy entrepreneurs you get on with. This can be a real danger to your business. According to an employment consultant:

> *You can't all be bright colourful characters in the business – you need the 'magnolia majority' who will actually carry out the work.*

It seems rather dismissive, but there is a point that you cannot all be charging in different directions. It doesn't matter how great your sales, if someone is not checking quality, or chasing late invoices, you'll go bust.

How to find talented people

Your potential employee is one of the most significant investments you will make. It's worth taking a bit of time to make sure you get the right person.

You should approach this in exactly the same way as you would your sales process.

1. Start with who you know. Ask around friends and family. Offer an incentive for people who recommend good staff. However, don't just stop here because it is safe and cheap. If you get the wrong person, it will be neither.

2. Approach local enterprise companies, careers offices and the like. They might have placement schemes to help.

3. Be flexible. You can find excellent candidates in groups such as new graduates, women returning to the workplace after having children, and retired people looking for work. You will be more than rewarded with their dedication and enthusiasm.

> *A proud new mother brought her baby to an interview. Great, I thought, we are modern and open employers – until she started breast-feeding halfway through the inter- view. I sat staring straight into her eyes, not daring to look anywhere else, like a startled rabbit caught in headlights.*

4. Keep in touch with your competitors, and in particular their staff.

5. Consider advertising, but don't just go for the obvious choices. If you're looking for a young and lively new member of staff, a local entertainment listings guide might be a better, and cheaper, option than newspapers. Also look at employment websites.

6. Always be looking. If you have a website, have details of whom to contact for job enquiries. Also keep previous CVs – the applicants might be worth keeping in touch with.

♟ Entrepreneur's Secret: Beware of employing your friends and family
It can be *extremely* tempting to do this. You think you know them well, it saves you the bother of interviewing and advertising, you

can have a good laugh at the same time, and you might be helping them out of a boring job.

For a start – it will make them feel devalued. From the moment they walk in the door, in the back of their mind they'll be thinking 'She only employed me because I'm a mate'. You will also have little time for friendly chats like you used to. Think how hard it will be to discipline them if it's not working out?

If you are determined to do this, at least go through a formal interview process, and consider other applicants.

See also 'Partnerships' (page 63).

The interview process

 Toolkit: **The form on the next page will help you conduct interviews. There is a template on the website (www.fromacorns.com).**

Step One: Write a job description. When doing this, resist just listing the *tasks* the person will have to do, but instead think of the *attitudes* they will need. If they are going to serve customers in your sandwich shop, a pleasant friendly personality is more important than food-handling skills. Conversely, if someone is going to oversee your production process, a close attention to detail is more important than the fact you hit it off with them. Other attitudes to consider are the ability to work under pressure, whether they are self-motivated and not going to need constant attention, and whether they fit with your 'culture'.

Step Two: Prior to the interview think through and write down the questions to ask which will get the person to open up. Like sales, you need open-ended questions such as:

- 'What type of work environment do you like?'
- 'What aspects of your last job did you most and least enjoy?'
- 'What type of job would you like to be doing in five/ten years?'

If you ask, 'Are you reliable?' only a muppet would say 'No'.

Job description	Shop assistant
Person interviewed	Jennifer Hopeful
Attitudes needed	Friendly and likes working with people Reliable – will turn up on time Previous shop experience Enthusiastic – will muck in
Notes	

Score out of ten	Friendly	Reliable	Experience	Enthusiastic

Step Three: The interview. Your objective is to make the interviewee feel as comfortable and relaxed as possible. This is not just being 'nice'. You want them to be as natural as possible so you get an accurate picture of what they are like.

Also, bear in mind that if this is a really good potential recruit, you're going to have to sell to them. Spend a bit of time at the start giving them the background to your business and selling them on your vision.

As well as working through your questions, it can be helpful to give them a test. In some technical positions you will want to check that their skills are as good as they say they are. It also gives you a chance to see what they are like in a working environment.

Step Four: Immediately after the interview, sit down and rate the person. It is tempting to go for a generalised impression, so force yourself to go through your form and be objective, giving them a score out of ten for each of their attitudes and aptitudes. Then you can weight them according to how important they are to you.

Step Five: Ask for referees and follow them up. You would think this is just a formality, but you'd be surprised. Either people can't find suitable referees, or have to go so far back in their career you begin to wonder. Or, the people you contact are somewhat less than enthusiastic.

How to be a good boss

Once you've got good talent in your business, you have to work hard to keep them fired up, and stop them going elsewhere. There are a number of steps to this:

1. Delegate

> **If it is painful and scary – then you are really delegating**

One of the hardest and most important tasks you will face in building your business is delegation. There is no magic secret to it.

> *A friend's father built up a large and successful retail business with many staff. My friend was over from America with his new wife on a brief holiday. For the two days they spent with his dad, every five minutes there would be a phone call from a staff member checking something trivial like a carpet colour.*

Imagine you are watching a staff member serving a customer. They aren't doing it the way you like to do it, so you stride over and do it yourself. By doing this, you have done the job to your satisfaction, and possibly quicker. You have also achieved the following:

- Completely demoralised the person doing the job, and told them you don't have confidence in them.
- Shown them there is no point in them making their own decisions, or taking responsibility for their actions.
- Shown the customer you don't trust your staff (so why should they?).

And who says your way is the right way anyway?

However, if you delegate complete responsibility (rather than just a task), you will find your staff are far more motivated. They will take control of a whole area of the business, completely freeing you up.

My father gave me a great piece of advice that I didn't really understand at first (apparently it's from Voltaire):

The best is the enemy of the good

If you are obsessed with every job that you and your staff do being perfect, there are so many other brilliant opportunities you will miss out on.

A reader, Al, sent me this quote from General Patton (US army general in the Second World War) that puts it into context (for 'war' read 'business' obviously):

> *"Don't delay. The best is the enemy of the good. By this I mean that a good plan violently executed now is better than a perfect*

plan next week. War is a very simple thing, and the deter-mining characteristics are self-confidence, speed and audacity. None of these things can be done perfectly, but all can be done good."

2. Reward them

The best rewards aren't always cash. By joining a small and growing business, a person might get more responsibility, experience, recognition, flexibility, variety, training and room to grow than in a large business. This might mean you don't have to pay them as much as your larger competitors.

They should also share in the successes of the business. This can be in the form of an end-of-year bonus or party, a sales commission or even a stake in the business.

3. Talk to them

This sounds obvious, but it doesn't always happen. At least every six months you should have a scheduled chat with each person. This is a chance to talk about how they've done, the areas they might like to improve on, develop or have more training in. It's also a great chance to listen to how they think the business is doing, and areas you should improve.

4. Inspire them

If you want to build a ship, don't drum up the men to gather wood, divide the work and give orders. Instead, teach them to yearn for the vast and endless sea. (Antoine de Saint-Exupéry, The Wisdom of the Sands)

Entrepreneurs can be the best – and the worst – people to work for.

By sharing your strong and convincing vision and passion in where you are going you can instil great willingness in others to follow you. Management consultants McKinsey talk about the 'sun-flower principle' – where all heads in the business turn towards the inspirational leader.

And if you're really lucky, this can almost make up for your impatience, disorganisation, lack of delegation and recognition, unreliability, etc., etc.

When a staff member leaves

It will happen – brace yourself. The first time it happens it will feel like you've been dumped.

> *My first employee left after a grand total of five days for a better-paid job. For the next week or so, I lay awake at night worrying to myself, 'Was it something I'd said? Should I have tried harder?' Finally, I had to draw a line at standing outside his new employer's office wondering what he had seen in them.*

Bear in mind, it may not be your fault. Try to find out exactly what the reason is, so it doesn't automatically happen to the next person. Also, try to get them to leave on good terms. The last thing you want is an ex-employee running around telling people what you got up to at the Christmas party.

Recruiting sales baboons

In the animal kingdom, sales people are the baboons. They're energetic, curious, mischievous, and they spend a lot of time striding around with puffed chests, admiring each other's lovely red bottoms. Before you take offence, I include myself firmly in this category.

Sales people can be highly annoying to employ. They can be cheeky, prone to exaggeration, rude, greedy, arrogant, impatient. Yet, without them, your business will never grow.

> *A sales guy worked very successfully for a publishing company and, after a while, was rewarded with a Porsche. Soon he bored of this, and announced to his bosses that actually he wanted a Lamborghini. After much heartache they bought him one. They unwrapped it for him in the car park, and went to swap the keys with his Porsche. The guy said, 'Who said anything about "swap"?' Their pride meant they had to let him go. He promptly went on to set up first one £40 million publishing company, and his new one is now up to £10 million.*

However, hiring and motivating good sales people can be very tricky to do well.

1. Finding them

If a sales person is good, they should be doing well in a good position. If they're sitting on the open market, or approaching you, some alarm bells should ring.

As with the search for new customers, a good way to find new sales people is to look for *change*. They might be moving location, their business might be changing, they might be returning to work after having children.

Otherwise you are going to tempt them away from current employment. Perhaps they'll enjoy selling your product more than, say, classified advertising. Perhaps they're looking for more seniority and responsibility. I wouldn't be put off by a good junior – remember, you're looking for the right attitude. You can teach them about your business quickly.

They also might be looking for a slice of the action – equity in your business. I wouldn't necessarily be put off by this – after all, far better to have 75 per cent of a £1 million business than 100 per cent of a £250,000 one. However, make sure they earn it – set targets for sales at which their commission can be traded for equity.

2. Interviewing them

Almost by definition, sales people are good convincers, so they're going to do well in an interview. However, what you are looking for is someone who can consistently pick up the phone and cold-call for new leads for you. That drive is much harder to assess in interview.

Ask for evidence: quiz them in some detail about their success in their previous job. Find out about the bonuses they earned. An experienced sales entrepreneur, Mark, gave me the following advice:

> *Ask them for their last payslips from their previous job – that will prove their success. Tell them you will be taking up their references, so they're less likely to make up stories. Finally, I always record the interviews. I find this makes them far more cautious about over-exaggerating their abilities as there will be a record of what they claim.*

You could also set them a test of cold calling, or try some psychometric personality tests.

If they look like the dream candidate, but they're not keen to leave their current business as they're doing so well (which is a good sign), Mark has this last piece of advice.

I phone a local car dealership, and ask them to bring a new car round. As we leave the interview, I walk them past it and say, 'The keys to this are yours if you sign up today'. It shows we're serious, it helps seal the deal, and it's affordable: a car on lease costs £300 a month. That's nothing compared to what a good sales person should bring in.

3. Rewarding and motivating them

 Cash never offends

For all their faults, sales baboons are simple creatures. Make sure their pay scale is performance-related, so they get a low basic but high commission on what they sell. This should also be an escalator, so they get a greater proportion the more they sell.

The sales might take a while to come in, so you might look for other evidence that they're filling the sales funnel: appointments made and leads generated. You can use the same sales funnel template on **www.fromacorns.com**.

If they're delivering on the business, then I wouldn't give them a hard time about time-keeping. You can also buy them nice shiny gadgets to keep them amused. And I'd try to keep them away from your other staff.

CHAPTER 23

Your growth strategy

Your growth strategy

Your business is up and running. You have money coming in. You know where most of it is. It's now time to pick your business plan out of the bin, and have another read through it. It is time to think if you are following the right strategy to grow your business.

I know 'strategy' seems a big word for a small business, but even if you only sketch out your thoughts on the back of a fag packet, it is vital you keep rethinking where your business is going. A common problem is:

Small business owners spend too long in the engine room and not enough time on the bridge

If the story of Shell at the start of the book says anything, it is how successful businesses have to change and adapt to customer demand. Consider the following:

> *Not long ago, an accountancy graduate from Strathclyde University found himself unable to get a job. He'd been turned down by the major firms, and a number of minor ones as well. He therefore decided to start a business from his dad's garage. He thought there was a market in training shoes. With tongue in cheek, he wrote to a number of department stores stating he was a fast-expanding footwear company and asked for space in their stores. Three of them accepted, and for many months he would drive around the country delivering to these, and catching a few hours of sleep in the back of his old van among the shoe boxes.*

It worked, and with time he built this to concessions in about 40 stores. Only then did he decide to open his first own-brand Sports Division store. Things carried on well, and in 1995 he seized the chance to buy the ailing Olympus Sports. Three years later Tom Hunter sold his business for £290 million, of which he pocketed £260 million.

When talking about his strategy, Tom says: 'I never had a definite goal in mind when I started out, I just wanted to grow. There is a certain logic to business and our attitude was to take things one thing at a time and see what developed.'

Some simple strategy tips

Here are some important things to remember about strategy.

Be single-minded about your customers' needs: If this sounds obvious to you – good. Because there are an awful lot of companies (particular IT) that fall into the trap of what the SAS call 'Shiny Kit Syndrome'. They become infatuated with how lovely and shiny their product is and completely lose sight of why a customer needs it in the first place. And bear in mind, these needs can change quickly. So, a good strategy starts by checking with your customers what they would like in an ideal world.

In successful companies, strategy often comes from the front line, not the board room. No one is closer to the customers than the cashier who serves them. Who better to ask what they actually want?

Watch out for the Law of Unintended Consequences: The late great Douglas Adams, author of the *Hitchhiker's Guide to the Galaxy*, coined this law. He astutely observed how many technologies, and companies, end up doing almost the complete opposite of what they were intended to do.

For example, the PC came out of the space programme, the internet was designed as a civil defence network in the event of nuclear war (and is now ironically one of the greatest threats to national security). The BBC was set up by a bunch of wireless manu-facturers to flog more of their radios. More recently, look at mobile phones – a fortune has been spent on whizzy 3G technology, but the greatest growth has been in fiddly and clunky text messaging. The danger is that you spend too long locked in your laboratory creating your master invention, without checking what customers might actually want to do with it.

Give yourself time and space to get it wrong: It is highly unlikely you will immediately hit upon what your customers want, so start your business on the cheap, and give yourself time to find what your customers *really* want.

Share your plan: There is nothing like having to explain your plan to someone else to make it clear in your own mind. Don't catch yourself saying, as so many start-ups do:

> *I don't want to tell people what my idea is as they might steal it and go and do it themselves.*

Bear in mind, success is 1 per cent inspiration, 99 per cent perspiration. Don't overestimate how brilliant your idea is, nor underestimate how lazy other people are.

Getting good advice

To quote the entrepreneur Gio Benedetti:

> *Starting a business is often like trying to climb a Scottish mountain in your shorts and flip-flops, with just a road map to guide you.*

In starting a business, you are entering a very strange country. It doesn't have to be like that. Millions of people have been there before you. Many of them will have had similar businesses. Even those in completely different businesses will often have some valuable insight. There is no doubt in my mind:

Pick the brains of someone who has been there before you

Getting advice from an experienced entrepreneur is worth its weight in gold

Such a person is typically called a mentor, and is someone you *definitely* want to have. So, how do you get one?

How to hunt a mentor

Ask the bride to dance

I remember asking a new bride how she was enjoying her wedding. She said she was disappointed that no one would ask her to dance. It's the same reason supermodels often go out with, shall we say, appearance-challenged partners. Everyone else is intimidated so they don't ask. The following are some tips to help you find an entrepreneur to help you.

Stage One: Draw up a mental job description of the person. Think of the experience and the type of advice you need. Is it general advice about how to build a business from scratch, or is it insight into your specific industry or your local target market? For example, if you are setting up a café, chatting to someone who has set up a clothing shop in your local area might tell you more than someone who has run a McDonald's franchise in a completely different part of the country. Don't immediately think 'I want to be an entrepreneur, I must ask Richard Branson'.

Stage Two: Once you have a good idea of your dream mentor – ask around. Ask your family, bank manager, Chamber of Commerce, suppliers, business support organisations (see pages 207–10), clients. Even if it seems impossible, bear in mind the Law of the Seven Degrees of Separation – a theory that everyone in the world can be linked together in seven steps. Someone will know someone who knows someone. You just have to be clear about what you want.

Stage Three: Convince them to come on board. This is not just a matter of cash and how much time they have free – most of the best mentors will want to do it if you can really sell them on your dream.

There are, however, some rules to mentor hunting.

- Don't be afraid to ask. I am amazed at how many successful entrepreneurs say they would love to help out a young business, but no one ever asks them. Entrepreneurs almost invariably have large egos, and love to have them polished by passing on their wisdom to young acolytes.
- Ask them directly. Don't wistfully stare at the ceiling sighing 'Oh, how I *wish* I could find a mentor . . .' in the hope they'll offer. The worst they can do is say no – and then they'll probably feel so bad they'll recommend someone else to help you.

> *When starting out with his mobile phone business DX Communication, Richard Emmanuel wrote a letter to Sir Tom Farmer, founder of Kwik-Fit, asking for advice. He was startled when he received a prompt reply asking him in for a chat. They have since collaborated on a number of business ventures. Despite being one of Scotland's most successful businessmen, Sir Tom said people rarely ever asked him for advice. (It would probably be a wise idea if we all don't immediately pick up the phone to him.)*

- Don't ask them for money.
- Don't take up too much of their time. If someone is successful, their scarcest resource will be time. Don't try to overly formalise the relationship, and don't demand too much too often: 20 minutes worth of advice over a pint from a good entrepreneur can be worth 3 hours of advice every week from someone else. Similarly, don't bog them down with the small stuff – ask them the big strategic questions.

Why just stop at one mentor? There is no reason why you shouldn't get a range of mentors. A relative or a friend might be a good sounding board, as well as someone in your industry, and someone who has built a business. You will often find the greatest benefit is taking regular time to sit and think about your business and try to explain it to someone else.

Ninja mentoring

"I'm finding it hard to get anyone to agree to be my mentor."
(Vikki, setting up a PA company)

I get more emails about mentoring than probably any other topic in this book (apart from those offering to bear my love-children of course). So I've come up with a new approach I'm calling 'Ninja mentoring' and I know it works because people have used it on me!

The idea is to get people to become your mentor stealthily without them realising. In sales parlance, this would be called the 'presumptive close'.

Asking a relative stranger to mentor you is a bit like whipping out an engagement ring on your first date. It gets a bit heavy a bit quickly. Instead, don't ask. Just keeping calling or emailing them for little bits of advice when you get stuck. Perhaps even ask them for a cup of coffee after the third or fourth bit of advice. Before you know it, you've got a mentor, and they don't even realise.

Will they steal my idea?

"The person I asked to mentor my business said I didn't stand
a cat in hell's chance and instead should sell him my product
and work for him." (Frances, publishing)

Yes, you don't have to be a genius to read the subtext here, do you? Still, you can't blame the guy from trying to pull a fast one. But this is a common worry. I often get people asking for advice, but they won't disclose anything about their business. It makes it very difficult to help.

So, I wouldn't go telling the world about your new idea. And I wouldn't necessarily ask a direct competitor to be a mentor. But, bear in mind the following piece of advice:

Our only competitive advantage is being six months ahead of
the competition.

And this was from the chairman of the one of the top five largest banks in the world. Nine times out of ten, what will make your business a success is your ability to make it happen quickly. Don't become so precious about your idea that you stay locked in your bedroom all day.

Getting advice from professionals and consultants

If you can get such great advice free, why would you ever pay for it?

However, good specialists, whether lawyers, designers, management, marketing or employment consultants, have often had years of experience in a particular area. They can save you months of fiddling round. You should therefore be prepared to pay them accordingly.

True, consultants often get a bad press. But it is not so much that there are bad consultants as bad ways to use them. The problem is when they become part of the furniture, and you just rely on them as a (very expensive) crutch for making decisions.

Always use the best advisers you can, but use them sparingly and for what they are best at. When they have imparted their wisdom – get them out. This isn't overly harsh, as any consultant worth their salt will be keen to get on to their next customers anyway.

CHAPTER 24

Dealing with failure

Dealing with failure

Learn to embrace failure

That might sound a little heretical. But being an entrepreneur is about dealing with failure – it is an inevitable part of the creative process. As Thomas Eddison, the inventor of the light bulb, said:

Of the 200 light bulbs that didn't work, every failure told me something that I was able to incorporate into the next attempt.

However, in this country, failure is a dirty word. There are not many books on failure. People seem to view it as a contagious disease that you will catch just by talking about it. It's like the army who won't teach its soldiers how to retreat.

There are times when failure is good for you and good for your business. Hopefully, most of these failures will just be small ones. But it will be your ability to deal with them, and keep going, that will determine the success of your business.

Even Richard Branson, before he hit big success with his record label and airline, worked through a range of businesses including a student newspaper, a mail-order record business, and family planning clinics. He just kept moving.

Write this on the wall in front of you at your office:

 Our greatest glory is not in never falling, but in rising every time we fall (Confucius)

Should I give up?

"I started with great enthusiasm in my business, and had a tough first year. However, I'm now in my second year of business, and it's still not working. Should I give up?" (Christina)

It's the hardest email to receive from a reader. Of course our natural reaction is to shout from the sidelines – don't give up! You can make it! However, clearly something is not going right in her business, and it's time to take stock. I would say there are two types of 'failure':

1. When it's time to sacrifice the sacred cow

As a philosophical Danish co-worker once told me, 'You sometimes have to be prepared to sacrifice the sacred cow'. You have to face the fact that one part of your business, which you have sweated many hours into, has no viable long-term future and is actually holding the rest of your business back. When this happens, you have to have the guts to stop this bit and focus on the rest of your company.

The spectacular story of Shell at the start of this book shows how a company went from a 'failed' small antiques shop to the largest retailer in the world. Similarly, Sir Tom Farmer started up a cooker-cleaning business in Edinburgh. Only by moving on from this could he start Kwik-Fit, which he grew into a billion-pound business.

So, if you are in Christina's position, you should look at your offering and mix it up a bit. Perhaps try offering your same product to a different audience. Or tweak the way you deliver the product, so you perhaps rent it, or offer consultancy rather than sell outright.

A painful example:

I started a yearbook business. It was OK, but after three years or so, the profits weren't really growing, and the business was very seasonal. So we diversified into being a publishing agency and grew rapidly. However ...

I noticed last year, three young students in America started a yearbook business, but did it online. Now they've received a $1 billion offer from Yahoo for the business.

Nice piece of diversification there Caspian.

2. When it feels like death by a thousand cuts

There will be many times when no matter how much you believe in the long-term success of your business, it will feel like you are continually failing.

Perhaps one of your major customers goes bust, a staff member leaves for a better job, you get a break-in, a competitor wins a great piece of work, and you get a bad cold.

Taken individually, these things wouldn't faze you too much. But taken together, the drip, drip, drip of negative feedback starts to drain the water from the well of your self-esteem. One morning you wake up and think, 'Blow this this for a game of soldiers' and consider packing it all in. As reader Gill emailed me:

> "Any advice for how do I stop the b*****ds grinding me down?"

This is *not* a time to give up! It's time to take some medicine for your mojo. Read the next chapter.

Vampire businesses

There is in fact a third type of 'failure'. Very few people recognise it because, ironically, it is masked by their success. I'll describe a typical example.

> Derek has been running his business for six years. While profitable, they've not grown much in the last couple of years. He is working six days a week, and late into the evenings. A staff member left recently and is earning more with a competitor than Derek is paying himself. He can't put prices up as he has lots of competition. He doesn't want to give up as he's put so much effort into the business, but no-one will buy them as the business is largely him.

Without realising it, Derek has created a business that he no longer owns – it owns him.

A great book to read in this situation is *The E-Myth* by Michael Gerber. It explains how owners should spend more time working 'on their business' rather than 'in their business'. They need to give themselves some space and time looking at the structure of the business, and how it works, rather than just doing a job.

While it's painful to accept your business is not going anywhere after all the effort you've put in, throwing more effort at it is not going to change that. You also have to consider your 'opportunity cost'. The real cost of you working in one business is the increased revenue you could be earning in an alternative one. What a dull world it would be if Richard Branson was only known to a few as 'Britain's leading student newspaper publisher'.

Mojo medicine

Mojo medicine

This chapter is longer than many of the others such as legal and tax. It's also not a chapter you'll find in many other business books. I make no apologies for this. Your mental wellbeing, motivation, happiness and health are some of the most important factors in the success of your business. So there's no point leaving this to chance.

How do you keep your mojo in top condition?

What makes happiness?

A ridiculous question I know. But there's been a lot of research done into the 'science of happiness'. One interesting research exercise into Lottery winners came up with three ingredients:

1. an absence of worry, such as about health or money
2. a sense of mission and purpose in your life
3. close connection with family and friends.

Surprisingly, Lottery winners didn't always do well. They swapped money worries for security worries. They often lost their goals in life, and many of their previous friends drifted away.

But, as an entrepreneur, your mission is very clear. What you have to do is avoid isolation from friends, and try to learn to switch off the stress.

Surround yourself with supporters

"I have an email from a friend that just reads 'WINNER!'. I'm going to put it next to my computer for when I'm next having a mini-nervous breakdown along the way!" (Dawn, product designer)

Isolation is a danger for entrepreneurs. You are working on your own on a rainy day, and a customer gives you a hard time. Without anyone to share the misery with, it's not much fun. But if you talk to others, you'll find they've been through exactly the same.

Try to surround yourself with positive people who believe in you. A good source is other people who have started in business. They will understand intimately the problems you are facing, and can share the horror stories. You don't have to meet them physically, just a phone call or an email is enough sometimes when you've got a problem you want to talk through.

You can join an online networking group. There are also many regional networking groups that can help you with this, and often informal 'curry clubs'. There is a list of support organisations on pages 207–10. If you can't find one – why not start one?

Try to find time for your friends. It might seem like a luxury when you're working long hours on the business, but it's a great investment. As the Americans say, 'Work hard, play hard!'

Take a break - throw a sickie

A wiser man than me once said, 'You cannot plan for pleasure'. So if a lunch goes on too long, or the weekend is just too good to end – what the hell. What's the point of running your business if you can't go on the odd unexpected bender? It also feels much more pleasurable when you know everyone else is commuting to their offices.

Let your philosophy be that of that great modern thinker, Ferris Bueller:

Life moves pretty fast. If you don't stop and look around once in a while, you might miss it. (Ferris Bueller's Day Off)

> **Success is a long hike rather than a quick sprint**

There is a real macho tendency with small business owners. Put a group together and soon you'll hear:

> *'I work a 10-hour day.' 'Well I work a 12-hour day, and do this 6 days a week.' 'Oh, that's nothing. I work a 20-hour day, and when I get home, I go for a 2-hour run and my last holiday was a 10-hour break in 1987.' ... (Apologies Monty Python)*

You simply cannot work 15 hours a day, 6 days a week, 12 months a year without (a) becoming a complete basket case or (b) ending up really hating your work. In fact, psychologists have shown you can only really concentrate effectively for 40 minutes at a time.

So for goodness' sake, give yourself a break. Heed the motto of Ru Paul, a 6 ft 6 in. former American football star turned drag queen, who took his philosophy from a motorway sign:

> *Have space, give space.*

It is very important for your business. Only when you have created enough room in your own life can you really listen to others, and spot the opportunities that might be there.

Go for a decent walk at lunchtime, or have a nap. My wife used to put appointments in my diary with a Mr S.K. Ives, and we'd nip off to a gallery.

Don't be hamstrung by a search for perfection:

> **The greater skill is not to finish every task, but to know which tasks you can leave undone**

Looking after yourself

Get fit: The Ancient Greeks had a philosophy of a balanced life called *kalos kagathos*. As part of this, they believed you should spend equal parts of your day working and playing sport. There is some value in this for the entrepreneur.

It may not seem like a priority to you, but exercise is a great way to get rid of stress, improve your concentration and handle the pressures of work. It should also stop you from getting sick.

You don't have to run a marathon, but as a general rule aim to double your pulse rate for 20 minutes, three times a week.

Eat well: Want to lose weight? Do your accounts.

Your brain is a real workhorse. It consumes 75 per cent of the blood sugar from the liver and 20 per cent of the body's total used oxygen. If you are concentrating hard, it is burning through 1.5 calories a minute, which is only half as much as a brisk walk. So if you want to think straight, you've got to feed it.

Don't skip breakfast, but look for a slow release carbohydrate like porridge or muesli. Snack on things like seeds and nuts, not lattes and doughnuts which will give you a short rush, then a massive sugar crash. Try to eat more at lunchtime, and then try to avoid a massive carbohydrate-fest just before bed.

Sleep well: Poor sleep impairs many functions such as memory and concentration. It's also been linked to a poor ability to make judgements. We've all had the '3.00 a.m. terrors' only to see how trivial it is in the morning.

I don't mean to be a nanny, but as someone who frequently gets sleepless nights, I've worked on a few techniques.

- Buy an expensive pillow.
- Take a short nap when you feel like it. The beauty of running your own business is that you don't have to stick to the nine-to-five routine.
- Don't exercise, have a large meal, or drink caffeine after 6.00 p.m. And bear in mind, depending on the individual, alcohol can work as both a stimulant and a depressant.
- Don't listen to the news. It's one thing being 'in touch'. It's another adding another layer of stress about depressing things you can do nothing about.
- Keep a notebook by your bed. If you are worrying about a problem, write it in the book, and vow to deal with it in the morning – not at 4.00 a.m.!

Don't hide under the duvet

If you are having problems, don't retreat under your duvet and refuse to speak to anyone. It may seem like a good short-term strategy, but your problems will not go away. However, you will find that when you confront your problems or fears, they are never as bad as you had imagined them.

Also, don't avoid making tough decisions that need to be made. To paraphrase Andy McNab recounting his experience in the Gulf War in *Bravo Two Zero*:

> *We may not always have made the right decisions, but the worst decision you can make is not to make any decision.*

Don't be good, be brilliant!

I have a personal bugbear with people, who, when you ask them how they are, say 'Not bad' or 'Mustn't grumble'. Why can't you just say you are 'Good'? It means the same thing.

Or to take it a step further – say you are 'Brilliant!' The amazing thing is, you will start to feel it, and others will be positively enthused by you.

The flip side – negativity – can be dangerously corrosive. Have you noticed how, if someone says you look ill, in about ten seconds you will start to feel ill?

Don't listen to the negative chat of others, and don't indulge in it yourself. If a client asks you, don't criticise your competition as it will reflect badly on you.

 I recommend attending a workshop, or getting hold of the material of Michael Heppell (**www.michaelheppell.co.uk**). He is a master of making people feel 'brilliant' about themselves. You might have an instinctive British scepticism of 'self-help gurus', but every pound I've ever spent on motivation and belief has paid itself back ten-fold.

It's not your fault

There is an interesting phenomenon in psychology:

If you ask the witnesses of a road accident to say what caused it, they will cite a whole range of external factors – the weather, light and traffic conditions. If you ask the driver, they will substantially over-estimate their own role in this.

This happens in business. If you are successful, everyone else will be quick to look at all the external factors – you were in the right place at the right time, or you got lucky. But if your business goes wrong then your overwhelming tendency will be to overly blame yourself, even if it was really down to external factors.

There are so many factors in making a business successful, and equally so many reasons it can go wrong. If your business doesn't work out, don't worry: it is not the end of the world. As Henry Ford said:

> **Failure is only the opportunity to begin again more intelligently**

Handling stress

There is a misconception about stress. Stress is not hard work. Real stress comes from not being in control of your environment.

Short-term stress in your business is not necessarily a bad thing. Having a period of working long hours to tight deadlines can be well worth it if you get a good pay-off and then have a break.

Long-term stress is the killer. This typically comes from other people having control of major aspects of your life. I actually think being an entrepreneur is one of the least stressful occupations, as you don't have to work for an idiot boss. Yes, it might all go pear-shaped, but at least it's all your fault!

Accept that there is a season for things:
There is a tide in the affairs of men
Which, taken at the flood, leads on to fortune;
Omitted, all the voyage of their life
Is bound in shallows and in miseries.
(William Shakespeare, Julius Cæsar, IV.iii)

Business, like all things in life, goes through seasons. You will grow in fits and starts. When it's busy, you will be wishing the work would go away. And then mysteriously, it does, and you are left wondering where it all went.

This is partly because when you are growing too fast, you are too busy doing the work and not filling your sales funnel with new leads (see page 112). It is also just the way the universe is.

If things are growing like topsy, don't assume they always will and so borrow to the hilt for a new sports car. Conversely, if things are going wrong, accept that this might just be a phase, and that success is just around the next corner.

Learn crying as a negotiation technique: The most important commodity you can offer your customers is trust. If you have made a mistake, admit it early, admit it honestly and admit it directly. Research shows customers are more loyal if they have been through a problem period with a supplier which has been successfully resolved. A genuine and heartfelt apology will usually defuse any situation.

Never say: 'At least things can't get any worse'

When I started off publishing yearbooks, I used to do all the typing myself. Finishing a book late one night, I didn't notice the spell checker had 'corrected' the name of the class president, Angus MacDonald, by taking the 'g' out of his first name. I shipped the books off to be printed in China and it wasn't until the graduation day that someone spotted the mistake.

I was mortified. I grovelled in humble apology, I offered to reprint the books, I offered to apologise personally to Angus. However, the students just thought it was funny and I got away with it.

Don't say: 'At least it can't get any worse: This will inevitably cause it to do so immediately!

Take a brave pill!

There is no doubt that starting a business is scary, but anything worthwhile in life generally is.

So go on, be bold, and take a brave pill.

I have the following postcard from a colleague sitting on my desk as I write this. It is a quotation based on the words of the German philosopher, Goethe:

*Until one is committed, there is hesitancy,
the chance to draw back, always
ineffectiveness.*
*Concerning all acts of initiative there is
one elementary truth the ignorance of which
kills countless ideas and endless plans:
the moment you definitely commit yourself,
then Providence moves. All sorts of things
occur that would never otherwise have
occurred. A whole stream of events issue
from the decisions, raising in your favour all
manner of unseen incidents and meetings
and material assistance, which you could
never have dreamed would come your way.
Whatever you can do or dream, you can,
begin it.*
*Boldness has genius, power and
magic to it.*

Go for it!

Useful contacts

Good business resources

Napoleon Hill, *Think and Grow Rich*, HarperCollins, 1995

Steve Parks, *Start Your Business Week by Week*, Prentice Hall, 2004

Michael Gerber, *The E-Myth*, HarperBusiness, 1991

Inc Magazine: **www.inc.com**

Sahar Hashemi and Bobby Hashemi, *Anyone Can Do It*, Capstone
  Publishing, 2002

Mark McCormack, *What They Don't Teach You at Harvard Business
  School*, Profile Business, 1994

Stephen Bayley and Roger Mavit, *Life's a Pitch*, Bantam Press, 2007

Paul Arden, *It's Not How Good You Are, It's How Good You Want To
  Be*, Phaidon Press, 2003

Motivational books and films

Ayn Rand, *The Fountainhead*, Penguin Books, 2007 (first published
  1943)

Tucker: The Man and His Dream (1988)

Jerry Maguire (1996)

Networking sites

Flying Startups: **www.flyingstartups.com**

Ecademy: **www.ecademy.com**

Business bricks: **www.businessbricks.co.uk**

Government support

The Business Links

There are 45 local Business Links operating across England. The

Business Link website is where you can find advice about government funding, grants, legislation and starting a business: **www.businesslink.org**

Scottish Enterprise
In Scotland, the service is provided through a network of Local Enterprise Companies. The Business Gateway is a single access point to a range of integrated services for businesses in Scotland. The website details start-up, growth and information services available: **www.bgateway.com**

Wales and Northern Ireland
In Wales advice can be obtained from Business Eye:
   www.businesseye.org.uk
If you live in Northern Ireland, try Invest Northern Ireland:
   www.investni.com

Other links
The Small Business Service: **www.sbs.gov.uk**
UK public services: **www.direct.gov.uk**
Her Majesty's Revenue and Customs (HMRC): **www.hmrc.gov.uk**
The Patent Office: **www.patent.gov.uk**
The Office of Fair Trading: **www.oft.gov.uk**

For young people

The Prince's Trust and the Prince's Scottish Youth Business Trust
Includes a directory of other young people started in business, hints and tips: **www.princes-trust.org.uk** and **www.psybt.org.uk**

Shell LiveWIRE
Help and advice for 16–30-year-olds setting up in business and a national business competition: **www.shell-livewire.org**

Young Enterprise, and Young Enterprise Scotland
A unique scheme to encourage and develop enterprise skills in students aged 15–25: **www.young-enterprise.org.uk** and **www.yes.org.uk**

Junior Chamber of Commerce and Junior Chamber Scotland

A Leadership Development organisation. Develops useful skills in their members so that they may excel in everything they do: **www.bjc.org.uk** and **www.jcscotland.org.uk**

For women

British Association of Women Entrepreneurs

A non-profit professional organisation for UK-based women business owners. Founded in 1954, BAWE encourages the personal development of member entrepreneurs and provides opportunities for them to expand their business: **www.bawe-uk.org**

Scottish Business Women

A real online forum where you find out about initiatives and events that can give you assistance, and benefit from an information resource that tells it like it is: **www.scottishbusinesswomen.com**

Business support groups

Federation of Small Businesses

The UK's leading lobbying and benefits group for small businesses. The website contains information concerning the key issues facing the small business sector today: **www.fsb.org.uk**

Forum of Private Business

A pressure group lobbying for members to change laws and policies for their future benefit. It also offers advice on problems such as red tape, employment law, health and safety and many other issues: **www.fpb.co.uk**

Entrepreneurial Exchange

Run by entrepreneurs for entrepreneurs, the Exchange is Scotland's premier networking group for entrepreneurs: **www.entex.co.uk**

British Chambers of Commerce

With 135,000 members, the British Chambers of Commerce comprise a national network of Chambers, uniquely positioned at the heart of every business community in the UK: **www.chamberonline.co.uk**

Institute of Directors

The leading membership organisation for directors who are responsible for the strategic direction of companies: **www.iod.com**

What's missing?

To: Caspian Woods
           Editions
           72 Newhaven Road
           Edinburgh EH6 5QG

Or email: **caspian@fromacorns.com**

I think you should add or change the following information in your next book:

_____

_____

_____

_____

_____

_____

I have found the following source of information helpful:

_____

_____

_____

_____

_____

_____

I have the following suggestions to improve your book:

_____

_____

_____

_____

_____

_____

Name: _____

Address (optional): _____

_____

_____

READ ON ...

Essential advice, inspiration, tips and techniques for every stage in starting up and running your own business.

THE ENTREPRENEUR'S BOOK OF CHECKLISTS

▶ 9780273712909 ▶ Robert Ashton ▶ £12.99

The only small business book to deliver fast answers in the form of handy checklists. Whether you have started up in business or are just thinking about it, this is the book that reminds you what you can't afford to forget. It's an invaluable source of reference at every stage of the small business journey and your checklist for success.

THE START UP SURVIVAL GUIDE

▶ 9780273708322 ▶ Chris Lilly ▶ £12.99

This book is your small business survival guide. It sets out all the common mistakes, errors and pitfalls entrepreneurs make in every area of business, and shows you solutions for the tricky issues that you might face.

THE BEERMAT ENTREPRENEUR

▶ 9780273704546 ▶ Mike Southon ▶ £12.99

You've got a bright idea that you think just maybe, could become a brilliant business. *The Beermat Entrepreneur* takes you through all the crucial stages of starting a business that is sound, lasting and profitable. It tells you what the other books don't – the lessons that most people have to learn by bitter experience and the tricks that all entrepreneurs wish they had known when they started out.

You can buy these books in all good bookshops, or online at
www.pearson-books.com

PEARSON
Prentice
Hall

READ ON ...

Get your business off to the best possible start with the UK's bestselling small business author Steve Parks.

HOW TO BE AN ENTREPRENEUR

▶ 9780273708292 ▶ £12.99

This is the ultimate guide to becoming a brilliant entrepreneur. It's packed with ideas, inspiration and practical advice to help you develop the attitude and focus of a top entrepreneur.

START YOUR BUSINESS WEEK BY WEEK

▶ 9780273694472 ▶ £14.99

Want to start your own business but don't know where to begin? Then overcome the challenges and turn your ideas into reality in just six months with this definitive week by week start up guide.

HOW TO FUND YOUR BUSINESS

▶ 9780273706243 ▶ £14.99

This is THE book to take the pain out of financing your start up! It provides the facts, figures and reassurances you need to choose the right source of funding for you and your business.

THE SMALL BUSINESS HANDBOOK

▶ 9780273695318 ▶ £18.99

This practical reference book is the perfect guide to running and growing your business. Filled with advice and guidance on all the day-to-day aspects of running your enterprise, it ensures you are well equipped to tackle every new situation that arises.

You can buy these books in all good bookshops, or online at
www.pearson-books.com

PEARSON
Prentice Hall